ENCHANTED WATERS

ENCHANTED WATERS

A Guide to New Mexico's Hot Springs

Craig Martin

PRUETT

PRUETT PUBLISHING COMPANY
BOULDER, COLORADO

Printed in the United States
10   9   8   7   6   5   4   3   2   1

Library of Congress Cataloging-in-Publication data

Martin, Craig, 1952–
    Enchanted waters : a guide to New Mexico's hot springs / Craig Martin.
        p.   cm.
    Includes bibliographical refernces and index.
    ISBN 0-87108-891-6 (pbk.)
    1. Hot springs — New Mexico — Guidebooks.   2. Health resorts — New Mexico — Guidebooks.   3. New Mexico — Guidebooks.   I. Title.
GB1198.3.N4M37   1998   98-39449
613'.122'09789 — dc21   CIP

Cover and book design by Kathleen McAffrey, Starr Design
Book composition by Lyn Chaffee
Cover photograph by Jerry McElroy, Pro-Visions; Ojo Caliente Mineral Springs Spa.
Interior photographs and maps by Craig Martin except where noted otherwise.

To my parents, Harry and Diane,
who taught me the value
of a day's work and a day's play,
and to always stay out of hot water

Contents

Acknowledgments

Thanks to Stan Davis, retired chairman of the Department of Hydrology at the University of Arizona, for sharing his insights into the history of water analysis and its relation to the mineral water spas of the past; to Fraser Goff, geologist at Los Alamos National Laboratory, for his infectious enthusiasm about naturally heated water and for setting me straight on how water gets hot in the subsurface and then finds its way back up to the surface; to the doctors at the New Mexico Department of Public Health for going out of their way to provide me with accurate information about *Naegleria fowleri;* to Bill Martin and Kathy Clark of Truth or Consequences for sharing stories about their town; to the former Isabelle Campbell for her stories about her father, Doc; to Elon Yurwit and Wanda Fuselier for passing on their historical background on Faywood, and for the loving care they put into their hot spring; to Rex Johnson for teaching me how to catch decent trout in the Gila River system; to the anonymous inventor of the Internet, who made it possible to locate obscure reference materials from the comfort of my study; to Arthur Olivas, archivist at the Palace of the Governors in Santa Fe, for his ability to instantly locate an historic photograph of anything in New Mexico, and for his persistence in assembling photographs of his hometown, Las Vegas; to Marykay Scott of Pruett Publishing for thinking of me, and for making it relatively painless to produce a book; and to Kevin Fabryka and my family, June, Jessica, and especially Alex, for sharing my hot springs adventures.

Hot Springs of New Mexico

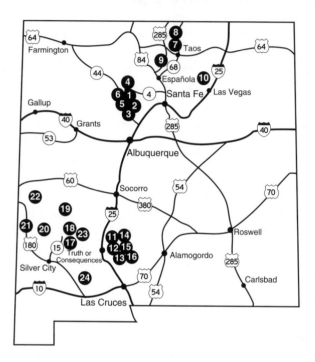

KEY TO THE HOT SPRINGS

1. Spence Hot Springs
2. McCauley Hot Springs
3. Soda Dam Hot Springs
4. San Antonio Hot Spring
5. Jemez Springs Bath House
6. Bodhi Manda Zen Center Hotel and Hot Springs
7. Manby Hot Springs
8. Blackrock Hot Spring
9. Ojo Caliente Mineral Springs Spa
10. Montezuma Hot Springs
11. Indian Springs Bath House
12. Charles Motel and Bath House
13. Artesian Bath House and RV Park
14. Riverbend Hot Springs
15. Marshall Miracle Hot Springs
16. Hot Springs Soaking Pools
17. Melanie Hot Spring
18. Lightfeather Hot Spring
19. Jordan Hot Spring
20. Turkey Creek Hot Springs
21. San Francisco Hot Spring and Lower Frisco Hot Spring
22. Frisco Box Hot Spring
23. Gila Hot Springs Vacation Center
24. Faywood Hot Springs

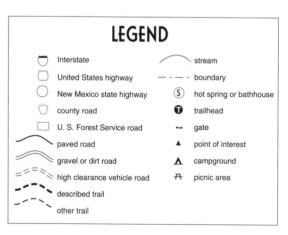

LEGEND

⬡	Interstate	stream	
⬡	United States highway	— · — · —	boundary
◯	New Mexico state highway	Ⓢ	hot spring or bathhouse
⬠	county road	🅣	trailhead
▭	U. S. Forest Service road	↔	gate
	paved road	▲	point of interest
	gravel or dirt road	⚠	campground
= = =	high clearance vehicle road	🕱	picnic area
	described trail		
	other trail		

SOAKING IN THE LAND OF ENCHANTMENT: AN INTRODUCTION

The shape and texture of the earth, water, and sky that make New Mexico are like the musical landscape of a Beethoven or the artistic landscape of a Picasso. They are varied, complex, full of contrasts, bursting with surprises, and rich in masterpieces. Craggy mountains, tortilla-flat basins, deserts, alpine meadows, weirdly eroded badlands, black rock gorges, and blinding-white sand dunes are all part of the state. Those fortunate enough to call New Mexico home quickly become spoiled by the embarrassment of natural riches that the state has to offer.

Hot springs are one type of masterwork in the repertoire of New Mexico. Like a complex musical work, the state's hot springs can be approached at many different levels. One can seek a spiritual revelation in thermal water, or a mystical experience that can bring a new approach to life. Many visitors look at mineral water as part of a holistic health regime. More superficially, but no less valid, New Mexico's hot springs can be a source of physical comfort, a warm, liquid wrap to soak out the tightness of your muscles, or simply a place to soak your tired feet. Because everyone attaches individual significance to hot springs, you will find them inhabited by a wide variety of people: New Age believers, naturists, grandmothers, families, hikers, backpackers, and those who simply enjoy the outdoors.

Hot springs are places to find healing or comfort, but that's not all. Foremost, they are intriguing freaks of the earth's geology, born of heat far below the surface. They are, too, pleasant destinations for a hike, places to spend meaningful time with your children, to share quiet time with good friends, or perhaps to make new acquaintances.

1

The United States Geological Survey database of geothermal anomalies lists seventy-seven locations in New Mexico where unusually warm water reaches the surface. About half of those spots have water that can scarcely be called warm, ranging from 75 to 88 degrees. Of the state's true warm or hot springs, all but twenty-four are on private land and closed to public use. The springs that remain accessible are a mix of private mineral bathhouses and pools, and hot springs on public land, which in all cases are managed by the United States Forest Service.

Writers have long discussed the cultural mix of New Mexico—Native American, Hispanic, and Anglo—and how the three combine to create the state's distinctive charm. For the scattered mineral waters, however, the charm lies not in the mixing of the peoples who used the springs, but in how the springs have been shared by each culture, each with its own similar purpose. The pageant of seekers at each hot spring has made the journey to find some sort of healing. The Apaches sought a spiritual cleansing in their sweat baths, the Spanish and Mexicans sought to heal the wounds of battle or the travails of overland travel by wagon or cart, and the Anglos came to the waters hoping for a cure for all manner of ailments. It is a common theme throughout the history of the springs that the special powers of the waters made each spring a sacred place and one that even traditional enemies could share, putting their hostilities aside as they partook of the mineral cures.

The land itself exerts a powerful influence on the people who live in or visit the state. The southern two-thirds of New Mexico fits best the impression that the outside world has of the region. Broad desert plains separate wrinkled mountains, the climate is dry, and there is plenty of sunshine. Many visitors find it a delightful surprise to discover that the northern part of the state is part of the Rocky Mountains. With high peaks over 13,000 feet, tree-covered slopes, and streams that support healthy populations of trout, this part of New Mexico is a remarkable contrast to the deserts in the south. Throughout, mountains and high plains prevail; the state lies above 4,000 feet in the south and 6,000 feet in the north.

One of the unique attractions of soaking in the Land of Enchantment is the predominance of open-air pools and tubs, both man-made and natural. The state offers seven indoor mineral bathhouses, commercial establishments ranging from simple to luxurious. The other seventeen thermal waters—including both developed and backcountry sites—are outside, under the sun and stars. Thus, enjoying hot mineral baths in New Mexico is most often an outdoor experience. The natural settings of springs and pools, along with the accompanying views of the New Mexican landscape, are what set these thermal features apart.

Hand and hand with the land goes the history of the springs, each of which has a story that may include Apaches, Civil War heroes, or conniving scoundrels. After a trip to one of the springs, you will come away with a sense of place that includes the environment of the spring and its position in history.

There's a more basic attraction to hot springs in New Mexico. Like the owner of one of the state's developed springs told me, "You don't have anything if you don't have the water." In an arid region, all water takes on exaggerated importance and a special fascination. Heat adds yet another dimension to water, and indeed gives it a mystical significance that people have appreciated down through the centuries.

People and Water: The History of Hot Springs

In what is now New Mexico, Native Americans who discovered hot springs in their homelands put the thermal waters to use. The springs of the Gila region were frequently visited by the roving Apaches. This tribe of the desert mountains used the springs to soak out the dust after long migrations on rugged trails and to heal wounds with a salve of thick, warm mud. Semipermanent villages were established near some of the more popular warm waters. The Apache fondness for warm water was well known to

An Apache family bathing at Ojo Caliente on the Warm Springs Apache Reservation (now closed to the public). (Photo by Dana B. Chace; courtesy of the Museum of New Mexico, neg. no. 57025.)

early European settlers: From the forks of the Gila to the Rio Grande, every spring possesses a legend of the warrior Geronimo bathing there.

To the north, the Anasazi/Pueblo culture found use for the thermal waters in the Jemez Mountains and along the Rio Grande and its tributaries. Several springs are decorated with intriguing petroglyphs that seem to carry a message about the soothing effects of hot water. There is some evidence from Jemez Cave near Soda Dam that the Pueblos used the nearby hot springs for ceremonies. Legends about the mineral springs at Ojo Caliente demonstrate the importance of the springs to as many as ten thousand nearby villagers. Geothermal springs around the Sangre de Cristo Mountains were also used extensively by the Ute and Comanche tribes, and the Jemez waters were frequently visited by the Navajos.

When the Spanish colonized New Mexico after the arrival of Coronado in 1540, settlers and colonial governors alike sought out hot springs to cure their ills. Spanish sheepherders were particularly fond of thermal springs to relieve the strains from the rigors of their outdoor lives.

When the first wave of Americans—mostly beaver trappers, commonly called mountain men—arrived on the scene in the early nineteenth century, they found hot springs a curiosity. After camping along the Gila River in 1824, James Ohio Pattie told this popular tale, a version of which is found in virtually every mountain man's journal.

> At night we reached a point, where the river forked, and encamped on the point between the forks. We found here a boiling spring so near the main stream that the fish caught in the one might be thrown into the other without leaving the spot, where it was taken. In six minutes it would be thoroughly cooked.

Across the Atlantic Ocean, the reputed curative powers of mineral water brought a surge of interest in Europe during the eighteenth and nineteenth centuries. The spa—a word adapted from the Walloon *espa*, "fountain"—became the favorite retreat of royalty and the rich. Vincenz Priessnitz, an early New Ager in nineteenth-century Germany, popularized the use of spas throughout Europe, and mineral baths soon became available for the masses. Many who came to the New World brought with them this interest in mineral baths.

Spas were part of the early American scene, and it has been suggested that the early hot-water resorts were politically important because they became meeting places where leaders from different colonies could sit together and talk about their common interests.

The Golden Age of American spas sprang to life around 1800. Early European-style spas were established in Saratoga Springs, New York, and Berkeley Springs, West Virginia. Visitors came to rest in the luxurious hotels, to soak in the naturally heated baths, and to drink the mineral waters that were reported to give health benefits.

During the middle years of the nineteenth century in America, dozens of competing curatives and regimens for health acquired large followings. From today's viewpoint, it seems incredible that intelligent people could fall for diagnosis and cure by phrenology, animal magnetism, or mesmerism, but in the absence of sound medical practice, where else had they to turn, except to bloodletting or purging? Water cures—the systematic application of cold baths—and thermal and mineral water cures are the most sensible of the early schemes for achieving good health.

As the nation expanded westward, increasing numbers of mineral springs beyond the Mississippi were transformed into resorts. In 1832, President Andrew Jackson set aside the nation's first federally preserved land, the Hot Springs area in what was then the territory of Arkansas. As the railroads crawled across the West, the railroad companies themselves developed hotel/hot spring combinations to attract tourists. An 1886 survey of mineral waters in the United States by A.C. Peale listed 634 spas and 223 springs used to bottle mineral water. Of these, more than 20 were listed in New Mexico.

Elaborate resorts surrounding thermal areas were built from Arkansas to Colorado. Hotel and bath complexes, from basic to high-class, came to life. In full Victorian splendor, the resorts were adorned in marble and tile, brass hardware, and gaudy statues. Every resort found it a requirement to publish a most detailed listing of the chemical composition of the thermal water. It seems that readers could be impressed only with the names of minerals they had never heard of before.

In the territory of New Mexico, thermal-water resorts were developed in the late nineteenth century. Despite, or perhaps because of the desert climate of the state, New Mexico never developed a world-class resort; however, high-class accommodations and bathing facilities were established at Radium Springs, Faywood Hot Springs, Montezuma, and Jemez Springs. The resorts rode a short wave of popularity until they nearly disappeared before the First World War.

As it was the sensible distrust of then-current medical practices that led to the popularity of mineral waters for soaking and drinking, so the medical community played a significant role in the decline of the American spa. By 1900, the establishment of sound medical treatments and training facilities for physicians brought back the public's trust in the practice of medicine. Fewer Americans sought a cure through water, and within twenty years, most of the elaborate spas were abandoned.

Hot Rocks and Heated Water: The Geology of Hot Springs

Those of us fortunate enough to live in the West have a tendency to take the presence of hot springs for granted, but in the world as a whole, geothermal areas are rare. Central Europe, New Zealand, and Iceland boast high numbers of thermal features. In the United States, a few scattered warm springs are found in the eastern states, but by far, the greatest number occur from the Rocky Mountains to the Pacific Ocean.

The rarity of hot springs is a result of the specialized geologic conditions necessary for their formation. It's not as simple as heating a pot of water on the stove, but the idea is similar. Required are a source of water, a huge basin of cracked rocks for a kettle, and a heat source that would turn all the pots in your kitchen to liquid. Fortunately for mineral-water lovers, the earth provides potential sources of such heat.

Depending on temperature, moisture, and the composition of the soil, a varying portion of the precipitation reaching the ground in the form of rain or snow percolates into the ground. Moving through the spaces between mineral grains in bedrock or through a network of fractures in the rock, water from the surface can reach great depths. Under normal circumstances, the water continues downward until the rocks are saturated or until an impermeable boundary is reached. Here the water table is formed, a subsurface repository of the precious liquid.

In most places, water in the water table flows slowly underground roughly parallel to the surface, occasionally reaching the surface to form springs, streams, or lakes. But in places where there is deep circulation of the water, a source of heat, and fractured rocks to act as a conduit for water movement back toward the surface, the story can be quite different.

Where bodies of magma—the molten rock of the earth's interior—squeeze toward the surface, there are two possible scenarios. First, the magma can find a route to the surface, create a volcanic eruption, turning the magma into its outer-world equivalent, lava, or other volcanic rocks. Alternatively, the magma can stay ponded beneath the surface, detectable only by deep-seated, low-energy earthquakes or by geothermal water reaching the surface.

A typical situation has a reservoir of magma sitting from 2 to 5 miles beneath the feet of the animals roaming the surface above. A small-scale magma batch might contain a cubic mile of hot material; a large magma body—such as the one responsible for the last explosive eruption around one million years ago of the Jemez Volcano—might be as large as 40 cubic miles. Water, along with any dissolved minerals it has picked up on the way down, is heated by the magma from a distance. Some additional water may be added to the system from the magma itself. The heated water becomes less dense and tends to rise. If the rocks above are permeable, or if there is a significant network of fractures, the rising water passes through the rock, setting up a convection current not unlike the movement you see in a pot of boiling water on the stove. The circulating pattern has precipitation feeding the system from above and the heated water rising from below.

Heat generated by magma is the sexy way the earth increases subsurface water temperature, and a single, concentrated heat source—even one several miles across—makes the system relatively easy to understand. However, in most geothermal systems (New Mexico's hot springs suitable for a pleasant, nonscalding bath fall into this category), the source of heat is not so glamorous. The extreme pressure and the heat released by the decay of natural radioactive elements present deep inside the earth cause

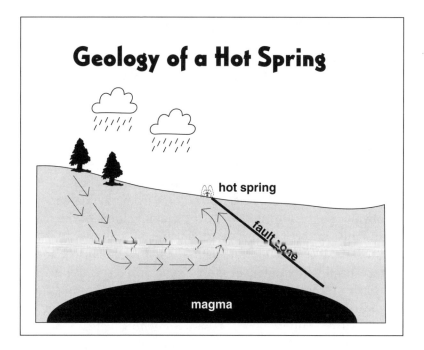

Geology of a Hot Spring

the interior to become hot. Instead of a well-defined, compact source of heat, thermal water can be heated simply by the high temperatures of the interior. This is particularly true in areas where tectonic forces create an extension, or stretching, of the crust. On a pizza, thin crust means more heat; so too for the earth's crust. The result is that in spots where the crust is thinned, heat flow from the interior is high, and if water can circulate deep enough, it will be heated and rise.

No matter which heat source is present, heated water works its way to the surface through fractures, an intricate, interconnected plumbing system. Most hot springs lie along linear features called *faults*, comparatively huge cracks in the crust where water can move freely to the surface. An impermeable layer below the surface can trap the water and cause it to move laterally, finding the surface where the barrier rock layer reaches it. Flowing from rocks onto the ground, water pools in delightful spots we call hot springs.

One additional factor makes thermal water special. Just as water in a saucepan can dissolve more sugar as it heats, the hot water on the way up to the surface has more power to dissolve minerals than the cool water on the way down. Thus, thermal water is rich in minerals picked up from the surrounding rocks. Depending on the type of rock it passes through, the water can dissolve small quantities of sodium, calcium, carbonate, sulfur, lithium, and a host of others. These minerals give thermal waters their special qualities, and they precipitate out when the water reaches the surface to form travertine and similar deposits.

New Mexico's geothermal waters come from obvious and not-so-obvious sources. In the north, the hulking dome of the Jemez Mountains is the remains of a once-giant volcano that last erupted about a million years ago. Magma remains close to the surface, heating the waters of more than a dozen springs.

More of New Mexico's hot water is a product of complex geophysical patterns that have combined to create a rent in the earth's crust of fantastic proportions. Stretching beneath the state and beyond, from El Paso to the San Luis Valley of Colorado, lies the Rio Grande rift, a place of tensional forces and crustal thinning. Essentially, the earth beneath New Mexico is being torn apart, forming a huge depression that has filled to depths of 30,000 feet with breakdown materials washed in from the surrounding high mountains. Along the edges of the rift, deep faults and the thinning crust have permitted magma from the earth's interior to well up to the surface, where a multitude of volcanoes dot the landscape. The rift's many associated faults provide an exit point for deep-circulating thermal water. The springs along the Rio Grande from Blackrock to Truth or Consequences were created in this manner.

The story is different down south in the Gila River Basin. The mountain ranges in this area are the remains of volcanoes that erupted as long ago as 45 million years. Little or no magma sits close to the surface, and it is the tectonic mechanism that produces hot water. Deep-reaching faults—leftovers from the period of active volcanism and more recent shifting in the crust—tap the heated water of the interior and bring it to the surface.

Health and Hot Springs

The use of hot water for relaxation or healing has a recorded history as old as writing itself. Warm mineral baths are discussed in Sanskrit texts from India dating from around 4000 B.C. Archaeological evidence points to the use of the mineral springs (and a segregation of public and private baths) at Merano, Italy, dating back to 3000 B.C. A century later, Greek physicians recommended baths to cure common ills, and the Romans had extensive mineral baths set up not only in their home cities, but in towns far from Italy.

Since the time of the Greeks, innumerable benefits have been ascribed to warm mineral baths. The claims range from curing the common cold to eliminating cancer. In the age of the great resorts, cures for almost every known disease were claimed by resort owners intent on luring customers.

With the rise of New Age healing ideas, most of the old and a galaxy of new benefits are attributed to hydrotherapy. Some claims are as farfetched as those made a hundred years ago: blood pressure reduction, improved health because of removal of waste products from cells, easing of arthritis, curing of skin conditions, and slowing down of the aging process. However, no scientific evidence exists to support any of these claims.

Still, who will deny the flowing of tension from tight muscles that are submerged in warm water? Warm water makes you feel good. In the simplest terms, isn't that all it takes to define a good soak? Although a soak in a hot spring should be a relaxing experience, one that sets your mind at ease, there are a few precautions you should observe before taking a dip.

If you have high blood pressure or a history of heart problems, consult with a doctor before visiting a hot spring or bathhouse. Seniors, those with diabetes, and pregnant women are also cautioned to check with their physicians prior to using a hot spring. Because children have a higher surface area for their size than adults, they should be monitored carefully to prevent over-heating.

Be aware that prolonged exposure to hot water can result in hyperthermia, an elevated core body temperature. Early warning signs include general weakness, slow pulse, and faintness. Severe signs are rapid pulse and hot, red, dry skin, symptoms of a serious condition that requires immediate medical attention. Many drugs, including antihistamines, vasodilators, narcotics, and alcohol, increase the body's susceptibility to this and other heat disorders.

Always take four simple precautions to avoid most heat-related problems: limit your continuous exposure to hot water, avoid all drugs, drink plenty of fluids, and monitor yourself for signs of heat disorder.

Avoid drinking untreated spring water, either hot or cold. This is especially true of any primitive hot springs you visit. The protozoan *Giardia* is present in almost all backcountry water. This parasite is transmitted when cysts from animal waste infect water supplies. Giardia can cause a severe intestinal disorder character-ized by nausea, abdominal cramps, and diarrhea. It can be avoided by treating all water by boiling or filtration.

A far more serious potential threat to hot-spring users is the amoebae *Naegleria fowleri*. This organism can cause a serious dis-ease, primary amoebic encephalitis. Nearly all cases, including one from the San Francisco Hot Spring in New Mexico, are fatal. (The 1986 case is the only one ever recorded in the state.) Don't be overly alarmed—the disease is extremely rare. Less than two hundred cases have been recorded worldwide since 1965 when the connec-tion between the amoebae and the disease was first identified.

Although this organism is found throughout the environment in air, soil, and water, most people who have contracted the dis-ease have been exposed to low-flowing, warm water, either in swimming pools, ponds, streams, or hot springs. The organism thrives in 82- to 104-degree water.

The amoebae can enter the body only through the mucus lining of the nose. Once inside, the amoebae migrates through the nervous system to the brain where it rapidly destroys tissue. Symptoms include severe frontal headache, high fever, nausea, and stiffness in the back of the neck and spine. No effective treatment is known.

Fortunately, the disease is easy to avoid. To minimize the risk of exposure, avoid getting water in your nose. Keep your head out of warm pools at all times. Avoid all low-flowing pools of warm water.

The New Mexico Department of Public Health does not systematically test either primitive hot springs or commercial bathhouses. The thermal waters featured in this guide have been carefully screened by the author, but conditions can and do change. Make a few quick observations before you decide to use any thermal water. Check for a reasonable rate of flow through any spring. Green algal growth is not a good sign. Use your best judgment when visiting commercial areas, and avoid primitive springs that are murky or filled with algae.

Hiking to Primitive Springs

New Mexico's thirteen primitive hot springs offer the unique experience of soaking in a wilderness environment. Scattered amid rugged canyons and forested mountains, these springs are the brightest stars in the constellation of New Mexico's thermal waters. Solitude, scenery, and a feeling of wilderness, which provide a direct link to the simpler days of the not-too-distant past, are the attractions of undeveloped waters.

A bit of effort is required to reach the primitive springs, perhaps a fitting prelude to the reward of a relaxing soak. You'll find hikes to hot springs ranging from a quarter mile to 12 miles. No matter what the distance, do some careful planning to ensure a safe hike.

Consider the distance and the amount of effort required to

reach each spring. Plan trips only to those areas that are within your ability to reach. If your physical conditioning is not the best, avoid steep climbs or long walks and plan to visit only the springs that lie close to the road. A rating of the difficulty of each hike is given for each spring.

All the hot springs in New Mexico are above 4,000 feet, and many are above 7,000 feet. Visitors coming from sea level will notice that the thin air of high elevation multiplies the energy required for even a short walk. Climbing steep hills is particularly taxing. When visiting springs in the Jemez Mountains or Gila River region, use good judgment. Slow down, which is an easy assignment if you permit yourself to take in all the details of the scenery.

On a hike to a primitive spring, sling a day pack or backpack over your shoulder and stuff it with a few essential supplies. In New Mexico's dry climate, carrying plenty of water is of prime importance. Intense sun, dry air, and high elevation combine to rapidly dehydrate hikers. When you feel thirsty, you are already a quart low on fluids. A good rule of thumb is to carry and consume at least a half a gallon of water per person on any day-long trip. Bring all the water you need, and never drink directly from a stream or lake. The universal presence of *Giardia*, a protozoan that causes severe intestinal distress, makes it necessary to treat water by chemicals, filtration, or boiling.

Your backpack should also contain some high-energy food, sunscreen, and foul weather gear. Warm clothing will help protect you against the evening chill, and especially in summer, always carry rain gear to meet the almost daily afternoon thunderstorms. Add a first-aid kit, matches, flashlight, and compass, and your pack will be well stocked.

Protecting yourself from the intense southwestern sun is important when hiking in New Mexico. A wide-brimmed hat is a welcome addition to your standard hiking gear. Apply a generous coat of sunscreen before you set out on the trail, and reapply every two to four hours.

Much ado is made of the presence of rattlesnakes and scorpions in the desert Southwest, but these venomous animals are easily avoided. Scorpions live beneath rocks, bark, and decaying vegetation, so to see one you almost have to go looking for it. However, after a soak in a hot spring, you might want to give your shoes a shake before putting them back on.

Eight species of rattlesnake are found in New Mexico, usually below 6,000 feet. With their secretive habits, they are not seen often. Rattlers are most active during the day in spring and fall; during summer, they avoid the heat of the day. You can usually avoid rattlesnakes by staying on established trails and keeping your hands off of ledges that you can't see beyond.

Large-scale maps are essential for finding most of the springs in the Gila region. The required maps for each spring are listed in the summary for each thermal area. Know how to read the maps before starting out.

Protecting Hot Springs and Their Surroundings

Like so many features of the natural landscape throughout the West, New Mexico's primitive hot springs suffer from being loved too much by too many. While the majority of users are careful to protect the valuable resource of hot springs and the public lands on which they are found, thoughtless users damage the landscape and degrade the hot springs experience for other visitors. Over the last ten years, several springs have been closed to public use because of abuse by those who profess love for the springs.

Protect the water quality of hot springs by keeping everything but yourself out of the water. Keep food, trash, and body fluids far from the pools. Don't bathe in a hot spring. If you want heated cleaning water, fill a container with flow from the spring and carry it at least 200 feet from the water before using soap. Make sure your soap is biodegradable.

Perhaps the biggest problem associated with hot springs (but by no means limited to them) is trash. Unsightly and unsanitary waste piles often grow near the springs, brought in and left by uncaring users. Walking barefoot at a few springs is hazardous because of the abundance of broken glass.

The solution is simple: Pack it in, pack it out. Remove all your garbage, and bring an extra trash bag to carry out trash left behind by others. Don't bury trash, because it will soon be dug up by the local wildlife. Leave all glass containers at home.

Special care is needed if you are camping near a hot spring. Set up camp at least 200 feet, preferably a quarter-mile or more, away from the spring. Your camp should be out-of-sight of any trails or other campers. Search for a previously used camp site and use it. Avoid trampling plants around camp by carefully selecting your tent site and cooking area.

Use only existing fire rings, or better still, cook with a fuel-operated stove. If you choose to build a fire, do so only when conditions are safe, not dry or windy. Use only dead and downed wood, and gather fuel from a wide area. In desert areas, where wood is scarce, fire is not appropriate. Before packing up, make absolutely certain that your fire is out, and make the fire ring attractive for the next campers so they won't feel compelled to build another.

Carry a trowel to bury human waste in a "cat hole" at least 6 inches deep. Select a spot at least 200 feet from streams, lakes, springs, and trails. Putting your cat hole in a layer of moist organic soil will speed decomposition of the waste. For more ideas on no-trace camping, contact a Forest Service District Office.

To ensure future access to a hot spring, leave it exactly as you found it. Vandalism to springs and nearby structures has closed several New Mexico springs to public use. Respect private property and stay out of posted areas. In clothing-optional areas, respect the wishes of other users. Keep in mind that "it takes a village" to preserve unrestricted access to public lands.

The Naked Truth

Although most primitive hot springs in New Mexico have a local tradition of clothing optional, hot springs have an exaggerated reputation for being the hangouts of those who want to bare it all to the sun and stars. Hikers, backpackers, and families looking for a relaxing spot seek out springs and enjoy them in the manner in which they are most comfortable.

Be aware that whatever the local custom, public nudity is strictly against the regulations on all public land. If you choose to enjoy a hot spring with your bathing suit draped on a nearby rock, you may find yourself holding a citation issued by the local ranger. However, the remote location of many springs and manpower restrictions of the Forest Service make enforcement of the law difficult. This situation may not last long. Forest Service law enforcement officials believe that as user diversity at hot springs increases, enforcement of the nudity regulation will soon become an important issue.

Bathers who wish to shed their clothes might consider a compromise, especially in the more accessible springs such as those in the Jemez Mountains. If all the bathers present agree to be nude, you'll likely have no problem. When other people arrive, you should ask them if they mind if you continue bathing without clothes. If they are offended or say they do mind, consider moving to another pool or grabbing a bathing suit for a while. The fewer complaints received at the district ranger's office, the more likely the springs will remain open to public use.

Names and Closures

Many of New Mexico's hot springs carry a suite of different names. You'll hear Manby Hot Springs near Taos referred to as Manby, Mamby, American, or Stagecoach Hot Spring. As you can imagine, this state of affairs has led to some confusion on the number and location of many of the springs in the state.

In this book, springs are given their most commonly used, correctly applied name. The first standard reference I used is the United States Geographic Name List, the official listing of accepted names and the names used on U.S. Geological Survey maps. If a spring doesn't appear on maps, I've chosen the prevailing name, the one that is most commonly used. Local names are also included. You'll find that once or twice I was forced to select a name that just made sense. In all cases, all the known names for a spring have been included in the summary table for each spring.

Avid hot springs visitors may be disappointed to find a few of their favorite springs not included in this guide. The truth is that past abuse by bathers has resulted in the closure of many springs to the public, both on private and public land. Take this as a word of warning: If a spring is not listed in this book, it is no longer open to the public. Landowners and managers repeatedly indicated that trespassers will be issued citations.

The limited number of hot springs demands that each user treat them with the care due such rare treasures. Visitors must follow the principles of Leave No Trace to halt the steady degradation of the land in the sensitive but high-use areas of springs. By following some simple rules, every soaker can help ensure that all springs will remain open for years to come.

HOT SPRINGS OF
THE JEMEZ MOUNTAINS

1. Spence Hot Springs

Location: Santa Fe National Forest in the Jemez Mountains north of Jemez Springs

Type: primitive springs in open pine forest above the Rio San Antonio

Services: none. Nearest services are in Jemez Springs, 7 miles south; basic supplies are found in La Cueva 3 miles north

Temperature: 106°F **Discharge:** 44 gpm **Elevation:** 7,360 feet

Hike Rating: moderate, but short, 0.5 miles round-trip

Maps: USGS Jemez Springs 7.5' quadrangle

Trailhead Access: From Albuquerque, take Interstate 25 north to exit 242 and head west on New Mexico Highway 44. In 26 miles, at the town of San Ysidro, turn right onto New Mexico Highway 4. Continue 17 miles to the town of Jemez Springs. From the Jemez Ranger Station on the north side of town, continue 6 miles north to a wide parking area to the right side of the road.

From Santa Fe, take US Highway 84/285 north about 15 miles to New Mexico Highway 502 toward Los Alamos. In 12 miles, bear right onto New Mexico Highway 4 and continue 44 miles to the intersection with New Mexico Highway 126 at La Cueva. Bear left to stay on New Mexico Highway 4 and continue another 1.6 miles to the parking area on the left.

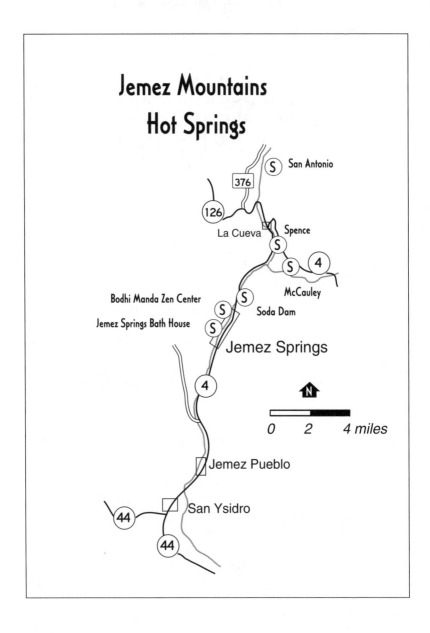

The back burner that heats the thermal waters of the Jemez Mountains is on a grand scale.

About 2 million years ago, magma from deep inside the earth found its way along faults bordering the Rio Grande rift and emerged on the surface. Over the next million years, the piles of lava slowly grew into a mountain of staggering size. At the time, the Jemez Volcano stood more than 15,000 feet high and may have been the highest mountain in what is now the lower forty-eight states.

As the composition of the magma changed to include more gas and steam, the eruptions became increasingly violent. Two massive explosions ripped off the top of the mountain and ejected so much magma from beneath the surface that what remained of the top of the mountain collapsed into the void. Left behind was the 10-mile-wide Valles Caldera, a much quieter mountain, and a hot blob of magma sitting 5 miles below the surface. That leftover magma is the heat source for the marvelous thermal waters of the Jemez Mountains.

Spence Hot Springs offers the best and worst of the New Mexico thermal-water experience. The springs flow from beneath a layer of shining, jet-black obsidian—volcanic glass—set high on the east slope of Cañon de San Diego. The Rio San Antonio and the Jemez River have sliced through the varied rocks spewed from the Jemez Volcano and created this pastel gorge with banded pink, orange, and tan walls. Under vaulting firs and spruce, the warm water of the spring pulls you into a peacefulness that matches the surroundings. That is, if you are lucky enough to find an empty pool.

A long history of abuse surrounds Spence Hot Springs. Twenty years ago, hot-spring enthusiasts built a small community of adobe and log huts around the springs and stayed throughout the summer. The homesteaders forced the Forest Service to limit access to the area to daylight hours. Even so, the surprisingly high number of visitors who lack respect for the springs and the surrounding forest leave behind tons of trash and broken glass each year.

If you seek wilderness solitude or a relaxed family outing, you should look elsewhere. Spence Hot Springs is a popular haunt in the Jemez area, and it receives heavy use in every season. One look at the parking area will give you an idea of how many bathers you can expect to find at the springs. Your best bets for a quality experience are before 10 A.M. and during mid-week.

Because it is difficult to find a time when the springs aren't in use, families looking for a chance to use the springs without others around will not have much success. Nudity is common and, although against Forest Service regulations, it is the accepted norm. The Forest Service does not recommend the area for families and warns against what it calls "inappropriate behavior."

Fortunately, Spence offers several pools to somewhat disperse the crowds. Thermal water seeps out in several locations from beneath a talus slope covering an extensive flat bench chopped into the steep canyon wall. At the main spring, the lower, larger pool can host a small wedding party, and the upper pool will accommodate a dozen soakers. The sandy-bottomed pools are ideal for spending a long afternoon. Water temperatures are higher in the upper pools and cool gradually as the water drops through a series of pipes and falls.

If you are willing to poke around a bit, you'll find several secluded pools—about the right size for two or three—tucked up in the conifers. Walk uphill, following social trails or outflow from the springs. Each pool has different characteristics of clarity, size, and water temperature. Most are in the area of a comfortable 98 degrees.

Although it's a short walk from the parking area to the springs, the hike is a bit of an adventure. A maze of intertwined trails head straight downhill, some ending on cliffs, others leading to dangerous mudslides trailing off into the river below. From the apex of the parking area, take one of the trails that angles a bit to the right; they are a bit less steep and will lead you in a minute or two to the west bank of the Rio San Antonio, a small trout stream about 20 feet wide. Walk to the left on the trail along the river, and you will come to a log bridge across the stream.

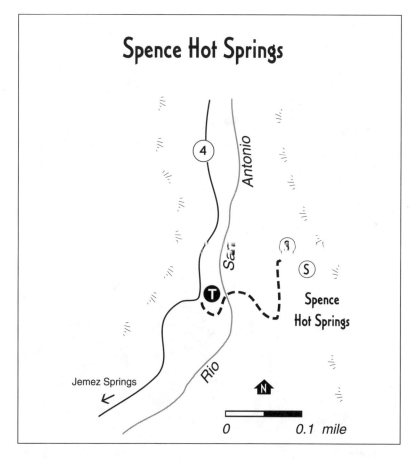

Spence Hot Springs

4

San Antonio

San

T

(3)

(S)

Spence
Hot Springs

Jemez Springs

Rio

N

0   0.1 mile

Once across the San Antonio, find a trail that leads up—
straight up. You'll soon come to the warm outflow stream dropping
from the springs above. The trails that lead to the right of the outflow are less steep, but whichever way you go, you'll find that the
200-yard climb gains about 200 feet of elevation and will take your
breath away. Any of the trails will get you to the pools in a couple
of minutes. The main spring is on the first bench to the left of the
outflow, but you'll find pools scattered throughout the forest.

Go slow and enjoy the scenery. The warm waterfalls are particularly picturesque, especially those formed on ancient travertine

These shady pools at Spence Hot Springs are ideal for an early morning soak.

deposits. Wildflowers are abundant in the wet areas, highlighted by brilliant red cardinal flower in late summer. On a more practical note, keep an eye open for the thick patches of poison ivy that pinch in against the trails.

Plan a visit to Spence Hot Springs for the daylight hours: The parking area and the springs are closed from sunset to sunrise. Overnight parking is prohibited. The Forest Service also advises that you lock your vehicle and secure your valuables out of sight.

The Jemez Mountains offer visitors not only idyllic hot springs, but a wide variety of outdoor activities. Hiking and mountain biking on the many miles of trails are popular activities, as is fishing for trout in the cool streams draining through the Jemez National Recreation Area. A visit to Jemez State Monument will provide an appreciation for the historical significance of the Cañon de San Diego. Campgrounds are located along Highways 4 and 126, and primitive camping is permitted off the main roads of the Santa Fe National Forest. Call the Jemez Ranger District at (505) 829-3535 for more information.

2. McCauley Hot Spring

(*Also known as Battleship Rock Hot Spring*)
Location: Santa Fe National Forest in the Jemez Mountains north of
      Jemez Springs
Type: a primitive warm spring in open pine forest
Services: none. Nearest services are in Jemez Springs, 5 miles south, La
      Cueva, 5 miles north.
Temperature: 85 to 90°F **Discharge:** 250 gpm **Elevation:** 7,330 feet
Hike Rating: moderately strenuous, 3 miles round-trip
Maps: USGS Jemez Springs and Redondo Peak 7.5' quadrangles

Trailhead Access: From Albuquerque, take Interstate 25 and New Mexico Highway 44 north and west about 40 miles to San Ysidro. Head

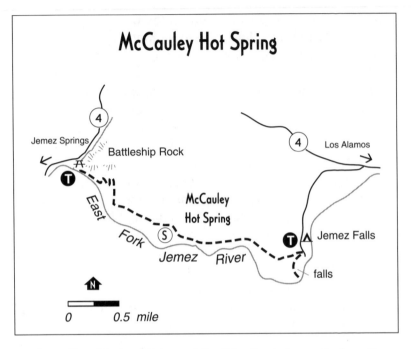

McCauley Hot Spring

north on New Mexico Highway 4 for 17 miles to Jemez Springs. From the Jemez Ranger Station on the north side of town, continue 4 miles north to Battleship Rock Picnic Area. From Los Alamos, take New Mexico Highway 4 west 31 miles to the village of La Cueva. Bear left, continuing on New Mexico Highway 4 another 3.2 miles to Battleship Rock Picnic Area. A small day-use fee is charged at the picnic area, which closes at 7 P.M. No overnight parking is permitted.

McCauley Hot Spring is a popular destination for bathers, hikers, and families. The large, shallow spring sits amid a picturesque clearing in open ponderosa pine forest. The location simply invites you to stop and relax for a while, enjoying the sunshine, water, and the sound of the warm outflow as it gallops down the slope, heading for the East Fork of the Jemez River in the canyon below. The water flowing from the ground is never hot, and this spring is more accurately described as a warm spring.

Happily, the length of the hike to the spring keeps away those less inclined to care for the area, and McCauley Hot Spring is cleaner, less crowded, and attracts a friendlier group of visitors than nearby Spence Hot Springs.

Nearby the parking area for the trailhead, Battleship Rock stands as a dramatic reminder of the volcanic origin of the hot springs in the Jemez Mountains. From below, the stretched-out cliff—tan rock, faced with streaks of green, yellow, and orange lichens—stands like the prow of a battleship. The origin of the cliff is clearly written in the rock language of the geologist. What now rises tall through the forest was once a narrow valley. During the eruptions of small volcanoes in the area, the valley filled with fluid lava that solidified into rock much harder than the surrounding one. As the Rio San Antonio and the East Fork wash away the adjacent rocks, the harder, more resistant rocks are left behind, making a mountain out of a valley.

McCauley Hot Spring has a giant discharge rate, a whopping 250 gallons per minute, and a small portion of the discharge can be seen stirring up the sand in the tiny pool directly over the main outlet. The outflow is ponded by a log-and-rock dam into a nearly circular pool with a sandy bottom that is nowhere more than 2 feet deep. About 40 feet across, this pool can, and often does, accommodate a crowd of bathers. The maximum temperature of the outflow is 92°F, but more often, the water is up to 4 degrees cooler.

About 100 feet down the slope, a second, smaller pool is fed by the outflow of the main pool. A large chunk of obsidian splits the flow into two channels that tumble into the pool. This second pool is 20 feet wide, 3 to 4 feet deep, and about 86°F. Another 200 feet downstream, a third pool that can hold two or three bathers sits beneath the pines.

Large schools of guppies and neon tetras swim the waters of each of the pools. Adapted to life in warm waters, these natives of South America were introduced into the pools more than ten years ago. Feeding on algae and leaf detritus, the fish have become self-sustaining, and the population has grown. They seem especially fond of nibbling on human leg hair.

"Ahh, that feels good!" Enjoying the warm water at McCauley Hot Spring.

Despite the walk in, McCauley Hot Spring receives it share of visitors, particularly on weekends when you may find more than twenty-five people in the three pools. Despite the Forest Service's policy against nudity, most bathers shed their clothes, but the lower pool is usually suitable for family viewing. If you are looking for a chance to relax in solitude and enjoy the sunlight bursting through the pines, arrive at the spring before 10 A.M., or try to make the trip during the week. To have this spring to yourself is a delightful treat.

Part of the attraction of this primitive spring is the pleasant hike required to get there. You can start at either of two trailheads. The lower, most commonly used trailhead is located at Battleship Rock Picnic Area. The spring is about 1.5 miles from the picnic area, and the trail climbs 700 feet to reach the spring. For those unaccustomed to the thin air at 7,200 feet, this hike can be moderately strenuous. The trail is mostly shaded, but it can be hot in

Languid pools tempt a hiker at McCauley Hot Spring.

summer. Deep snow can make access to the spring difficult from November to early or mid-March.

Trail 137, the East Fork Trail, begins just behind the imposing gazebo across the bridge over the Rio San Antonio from the main parking area at Battleship Rock. As you walk behind the gazebo, stay on the main trail close to the river. A maze of fishing trails branch off from the route, so watch for Trail 137 signposts to stay on the right track.

The trail steadily climbs the north wall of the canyon of the East Fork of the Jemez River. Winding through an open, airy forest of ponderosa pine, the trail offers views across the canyon to bold red sandstone cliffs mixed with dark green fir and feathery aspen. The East Fork shouts from below as it jumps over smooth boulders tumbled from the 1,000-foot-high slopes above. Several switch-backs take you up the slope and the soil alternates between gray and red as the trail winds amid giant boulders of sparkling obsidian.

After 1 mile, the trail turns away from the East Fork. In another half a mile, climb a steep, rubbly hill, then look for the stone outlines of a small Pueblo ruin to the right of the trail. Just beyond, the sound of running water announces you've reached the spring.

The alternate, upper trailhead begins near Jemez Falls and winds just under 2.5 miles to the spring. The trailhead is located past Jemez Falls Campground about 4 miles east of La Cueva on Highway 4. The trail begins at the parking area for Jemez Falls, splitting off to the right 200 feet down the Falls Trail. Starting at 7,900 feet, East Fork Trail 137 drops 600 feet to the spring as it follows the canyon downstream. The half-mile side trip to the falls is worth the extra few minutes.

Three Forest Service campgrounds are located nearby. Jemez Falls Campground is at the upper trailhead. Two miles west, Redondo Campground has over fifty wooded sites. San Antonio Campground is 1 mile north of La Cueva on New Mexico Highway 126. Backpacking into the spring is permitted and flat, shady campsites are plentiful on the bench surrounding the spring. Because overnight parking is not permitted at Battleship Rock, backpackers should start their trip at the Jemez Falls parking area.

McCauley Hot Spring is the most enjoyable primitive spring in the Jemez Mountains. To maintain the high quality of this experience and to assure continued public access to the area, it is the responsibility of every visitor to treat the spring and its surroundings with respect. Be sure to pack out your trash.

3. Soda Dam Hot Springs

Location: Santa Fe National Forest in the Jemez Mountains north of Jemez Springs
Type: a spectacular travertine deposit amid a cluster of small hot springs
Services: none. Nearest services are in Jemez Springs, 1 mile south.

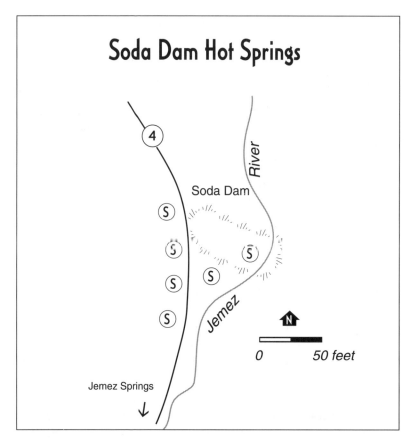

Soda Dam Hot Springs

Temperature: 92 to 118°F   **Discharge:** 60 to 106 gpm
Elevation: 6,340 feet
Maps: USGS Jemez Springs 7.5' quadrangle

How to Get There: From Albuquerque, take Interstate 25 and New Mexico Highway 44 north and west about 40 miles to San Ysidro. Head
north on New Mexico Highway 4 for 17 miles to Jemez Springs. From
the Jemez Ranger Station on the north side of town, continue 1 mile
north to the dam. Park in the wide pullout on the right. From Los
Alamos, take New Mexico Highway 4 west 31 miles to the village of La
Cueva. Bear left, continuing on New Mexico Highway 4 another 6 miles
to the dam and park on the left. No overnight parking is permitted.

Soda Dam in the Jemez Mountains is one of New Mexico's most unique geothermal features. A massive deposit of travertine that stretches from wall to wall of the Cañon de San Diego, the terraces once completely dammed the Jemez River. The river has worn a channel through the dam, adding a sparkling waterfall to the already arresting scene. Thin sheets of warm water flow over the face of the dam where algal growth paints yellow and green lines on the buff surface.

The soothing mineral waters at Soda Dam have long been known. Evidence of this lies in the abrupt cliff overlooking the dam. Halfway up the slope is a rock shelter, Jemez Cave. A rich treasure of artifacts was found there and showed that the cave had been used by big-game hunters more than two thousand years ago, followed by the Pueblo culture after the Spanish arrived in the area in the seventeenth century. A member of Jemez Pueblo told archaeologists in 1934 that for a long time the cave was used as a resting place by Jemez residents who came to use Soda Dam in ceremonies.

The name *soda* implies incorrectly that the extensive deposit is made of the chemical in baking soda, sodium bicarbonate. However, like other travertine mounds from Yellowstone to New Zealand, Soda Dam is composed of calcium carbonate.

The mineral travertine is a common feature of geothermal areas. Deep underground, as heated water passes through cracks in buried limestone, it readily dissolves small amounts of the calcium carbonate, the major mineral constituent of limestone. Just like sugar in a saucepan, the hotter the water, the more mineral it can hold. When the heated water reaches the surface at a hot spring, the temperature suddenly cools and the water can no longer hold as much dissolved mineral. As a result, much of calcium carbonate in the water precipitates out and is deposited on the flow surface as travertine. Because it drops out of slow-flowing water, travertine assumes an endless variety of wrinkled shapes, often forming stair-step pools.

In the case of Soda Dam, water from deep inside the Valles Caldera is heated by the magma below the volcano and flows

Boys from the Los Alamos Ranch School enjoy a day at Soda Dam in 1924. (Photograph courtesy of the Los Alamos Historical Archives, cat. no. R3434i.)

With its massive deposits of travertine, Soda Dam is one of New Mexico's most unique geothermal features.

toward the surface, passing through the limestones of the Madera formation along the way. (Geologists at Los Alamos National Laboratory have found the relative amounts of important elements dissolved in the water at Soda Dam match those from fluids deep within the caldera.) At the site of Soda Dam, the Jemez fault zone brings once deeply buried granite to the surface along a series of deep cracks. Where the cracks meet the surface, the heated water finds its way out from underground. Old travertine deposits sitting high on the west wall of the canyon demonstrate that the springs have been active for tens of thousands of years as the river has carved out its canyon.

Over the past one hundred years, the number of reported active hot springs in the Soda Dam area has varied from ten to forty-two. In 1902, twenty-two springs were located on top of the dam, all flowing and depositing travertine. It was these springs that built the dam. Conditions at Soda Dam changed, and in 1912, only eleven active springs were found there.

Up until about thirty years ago, springs along the top of the dam kept it growing. When the adjacent Highway 4 was built in the mid-1960s, engineers blasted away the western portion of the dam. This not only radically altered the appearance of Soda Dam, but it transformed the plumbing system of the springs. With a shift of thermal activity away from the top of the travertine mound, the dam ceased to grow.

Soda Dam is more a place to enjoy the unique scenery than to soak much more than your toes. All of the springs are less than 2 feet across, and the nearby pools are small too. At least a dozen of the springs lie in a line parallel to and only a few feet from the west side of the highway. Even these springs have their visual attractions from the bright green streaks of algae on their bottoms. Just above the road, hot water constantly spouts from a small hole in the rocks like a miniature geyser. Although traffic on the highway usually slows in this area, use plenty of caution when viewing these delights and always watch for children.

The most unusual hot spring at Soda Dam is hidden in a small travertine cave at the foot of the dam on its east end, just above the river. You can work your way into the cave on a few easy rock steps, and don't forget to duck your head. Warm water slides out of the spring, which flows from a bowl-shaped travertine mound. The odor of sulfur is strong within the confines of the cave. Again, use caution in this area and stay away from the ledges just above the river.

4. San Antonio Hot Spring

Location: Santa Fe National Forest in the Jemez Mountains north of Jemez Springs

Type: a primitive hot spring located in a scenic canyon

Services: none. Nearest services are in Jemez Springs, 20 miles south. Groceries available in La Cueva, 8 miles south.

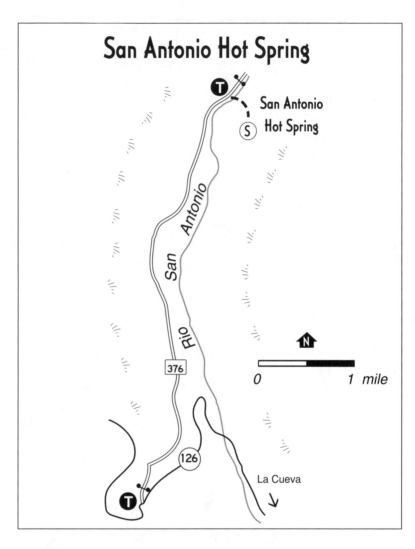

San Antonio Hot Spring

San Antonio Hot Spring

Temperature: 105 to 120°F
Discharge: varies from 40 to 200 gpm   **Elevation:** 8,360 feet
Bike Rating: moderate, 12 miles round-trip
Maps: USGS Seven Springs 7.5' quadrangle

Trailhead Access: From Albuquerque, take Interstate 25 and New Mexico Highway 44 north and west about 40 miles to San Ysidro. Head north on New Mexico Highway 4 for 17 miles to Jemez Springs. From the Jemez Ranger Station on the north side of town, continue 5 miles north to the village of La Cueva at the intersection with New Mexico Highway 126. From Santa Fe, reach La Cueva via US Highway 285, New Mexico Highway 502 and New Mexico Highway 4 past Bandelier National Monument. La Cueva is 35 miles west of Bandelier on New Mexico Highway 4. From La Cueva, head west on Highway 126 for 4 miles to the intersection with Forest Road 376 and turn right. When dry, this dirt road is usually passable to all vehicles. Continue 6 miles, taking the right fork that drops to a parking area near a bridge over the Rio San Antonio.

The Santa Fe National Forest Service office has a love-hate relationship with San Antonio Hot Spring. The spring has long been a popular destination in the Jemez Mountains, but frequent vandalism to the spring and the nearby Youth Conservation Corps cabin has caused the Forest Service to close the hot spring. The policy has changed several times over the last decade, and no permanent solution has been found. When the spring is officially closed, rangers levy a fine of twenty-five to one hundred dollars on bathers who are found in the pools. In order to avoid the fine for bathing in the spring, contact the Jemez Ranger District Office ([505] 829-3535) to find out the status of the hot spring.

When it is open to the public, this off-the-beaten-path spring is one of the most delightful in New Mexico. The vent sits in a small clearing 200 feet above the floor of San Antonio Canyon. From the relaxing pools, you'll have a commanding view of the canyon below and the columns of orange tuff that form the canyon's west wall. The grassy floor of the canyon gives way to slopes clothed in conifers, which are interrupted at irregular intervals by teepee-shaped mounds of ashen tuff. The scene easily fits into the way you'll feel while steeping in the thermal waters of the hot spring.

San Antonio Hot Spring is about 6 miles from the nearest pavement, but access is easy via Forest Road 376 and most of the summer requires but a short walk. This road, usually blocked by snow from November to February, is closed to motor vehicles

Tent rocks of volcanic origin are part of the enchanting scenery at San Antonio Hot Spring.

from February to about May 15 for resource protection. During this time, you can either walk, ski, or mountain bike to the spring, a 12-mile round-trip. The hike is long and can be dusty and hot, making a bike the perfect mode of transportation. Indeed, visiting San Antonio Hot Spring by mountain bike when the road is closed to vehicles is New Mexico's best mountain bike/hot spring excursion. When snow conditions are right, skiing into the spring on a crystal winter day will make a memorable trip.

To reach the spring when the road is closed (or when you want to earn your way to a good soak), park at the gate at the intersection of Highway 126 and Forest Road 376 about 4 miles west of La Cueva. Head north on the forest road, enjoying the undulating hills that make either biking or skiing a pleasure. On a bike, the ride in requires little technical skill, but the almost-9,000-foot elevation and the 400-foot climb back to the trailhead do require a moderate fitness level. On cross-country skis, the 12-

mile round-trip is physically demanding and can be done by skiers with intermediate Nordic skills. You can make the trip in a half day on wheels, but plan on a long, full day on skis. It will take about thirty minutes to get to the spring by bike and at least two hours on skis. Depending on winter snowpack, skis are practical from late November to early March, and a bike will work the rest of the year.

A small parking area is located on the Rio San Antonio at the end of Forest Road 376. To reach the spring from the parking area, walk across the bridge and climb steeply up the obvious trail ahead. The trail has many branches, all of which lead to the pools. It takes about five minutes of steep climbing to reach the hot spring.

You'll find five well-constructed, rock-bordered pools perched high on the slope above the canyon. The pools are terraced onto the hillside, with picturesque cascaded trickling from level to level. Water temperature is constant among the pools, each at a near-perfect 105 degrees. The sand and fine gravel bottoms are comfortable to sit on, and the rock wall lining each serves as a relaxing backrest. Add the colorful view to the perfect mineral water, and you've got a premier location to relax.

The upper pool is the largest—20 feet long, 10 feet wide, 3 feet deep—and will comfortably hold ten to twelve bathers. Pleasantly hot water issues from three pipes into the natural tub. The lower pools are crowded with more than two adults but are well suited for children. Although nudity is common, you'll find that the lower pools are generally used by bathers with suits.

The nearby cabin is used by the Youth Conservation Corps as headquarters when it is working in the area. Because of past experiences with vandalism at the cabin, the Forest Service has posted the area and visitors must stay out. Avoid a wrangle with the rangers and heed their warning.

Like the other hot springs in the Jemez Mountains, San Antonio has been known for more than a century. The Wheeler Survey noted the location of the spring during the first geologic reconnaissance of New Mexico in 1874. Since then, the spring has received a fair amount of attention from geologists at Los Alamos National Laboratory. For more than a decade, Los Alamos scientists drilled and studied a geothermal well just up the road from the San Antonio springs, hoping to learn more about the nature of the Valles Caldera and perhaps develop a way to harness some of the heat for energy production.

Although the Fenton Hill Geothermal Well failed to produce usable energy, it did contribute much to the understanding of the origins of the waters in the area's hot springs. For example, the spring water in San Antonio Canyon was found to be meteoric—that is, coming from the atmosphere. Levels of the radioisotope tritium indicate that the water spends more than twenty years underground before issuing from the spring. Because of the San Antonio Canyon's position on the edge of the Valles Caldera, the hot groundwater finds its way to the surface along the ring fracture zone that encircles the caldera.

Basic supplies can be found in La Cueva, where you'll also find a small lodge and restaurant. Primitive camping is permitted near San Antonio Hot Spring, but please observe regulations and camp at least 200 feet away from the stream. Bring your own water, or be prepared to treat the water from the stream. Developed campgrounds are located 5 miles west at Fenton Lake and 4 miles east at Redondo.

The upper valleys of the Jemez Mountains—such as those of the Rio San Antonio—are worth a visit even if the hot spring is closed to the public. Hiking along the Rio San Antonio is delightful with the resident deer and elk providing entertainment. Brown and rainbow trout are found in the stream, which is managed for fly-and-lure fishing only with a two-fish limit. Lake anglers will want to give nearby Fenton Lake a try, particularly in the spring and fall. The web of forest roads woven on the hills around San Antonio Canyon is ideal for mountain bikes. What better way to end a day of outdoor recreation than to relax in the soothing thermal waters of the Jemez Country?

5. Jemez Springs Bath House

Location: the town of Jemez Springs
Type: privately owned bathhouse in an historic setting
Services: private indoor or outdoor mineral baths, exercise studio, massage, cosmetology. Nearby restaurants, bed and breakfasts, and basic supplies in town.
Temperature: 154 to 186°F, mixed at the bath to preferred temperature
Discharge: 2 to 10 gpm   **Elevation:** 6,200 feet
Address: P.O. Box 112, Jemez Springs, NM 87025
Phone: (505) 829-3303
Web address: www.jemez.com/baths/

How to Get There: From Albuquerque, take Interstate 25 north to exit 242 and head west on New Mexico Highway 44. After 26 miles, at the town of San Ysidro, turn right onto New Mexico Highway 4. Continue 17 miles to the town of Jemez Springs. From Santa Fe, take US Highway 84/285 north about 15 miles to New Mexico Highway 502 toward Los Alamos. In 12 miles, bear right onto New Mexico Highway 4 and continue 55 miles to Jemez Springs.

Once in Jemez Springs, where the 25-mile-per-hour speed limit is strictly enforced, look for the Jemez Springs Bath House located at a small park near the fire station and library on the west side of the road. Watch for the signs on the main road pointing the way.

The lush bottom of the Cañon de San Diego is a striking contrast to the stark walls of stocky, widely spaced juniper and piñon pine. With its tall, cooling cottonwoods and ever-flowing supply of water in the Jemez River, the canyon has lured farmers since at least the fifteenth century. A half-dozen large pueblo ruins are found high on the surrounding mesas, the homes of the resident farmers. Tucked in one small side canyon just above the Jemez River are the ruins of Giusewa, a thriving pueblo when the Span-

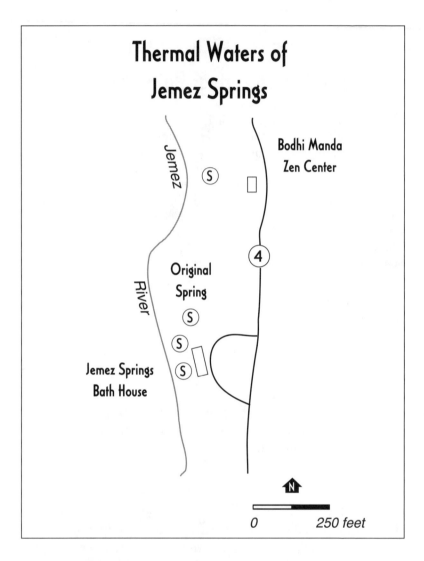

Thermal Waters of Jemez Springs

Jemez

River

Bodhi Manda
Zen Center

(S)

(4)

Original
Spring

(S)

(S)

Jemez Springs
Bath House

(S)

N

0   250 feet

ish first explored the area in the late sixteenth century. In Tewa, the language of the Pueblos, the name means "at the hot place" or "place at the boiling waters."

The hot springs among the red rocks of Cañon de San Diego have been used by health seekers for centuries. Foraging ancestors of the Pueblos frequently camped in the canyon and probably regarded the hot springs as a mystical place. The nearby Pueblo towns claim use of the springs since their people first arrived here in the fourteenth century.

The Spanish Rodriguez-Chamuscado expedition of 1583 traveled up the Jemez River and visited two pueblos, one of which they named Baños (baths). It is likely that Baños is the ruin known as Giusewa and was so-named for its location near the hot springs. In 1599, the Spanish colonizer Juan Oñate visited the canyon and reported back to his superiors in Mexico that he had found mineral waters that had healing powers. In spring 1658, New Mexican Governor Juan Manso traveled to the springs from Santa Fe to seek relief from an illness, accompanied by an escort of soldiers to deter an attack by the Navajos.

After the Spanish drove the residents of the nearby mesa-top pueblos into a new village in the valley—the current Jemez Pueblo—the Native people continued to use the springs. They were joined by Spanish ranchers, farmers, and traders who settled the Cañon de San Diego land grant after 1729.

When Lieutenant James Simpson passed through in 1849, he reported the name of the small village near the springs as Ojo Caliente. A sketch of the springs by Simpson's artist, Edward Kern, shows two steam vents, one of which is covered by a canopy of pine branches—a primitive bathhouse?

Locals of the small town Simpson visited in 1849 called their home *Ojos Calientes* ("hot springs"). In the 1850s, the first public bath at the springs was established by the Archuleta family. The town acquired a rough reputation in the 1870s when cattle rustlers and miners moved in. When the first post office was set up in 1888, the town's name was changed to Archuleta, implying that the family still operated the springs. The village changed its name to Perea before settling on Jemez Springs in 1907.

Geologist A.B. Reagan passed through the canyon in 1902 and found two hotels in town, each operating at one of the two groups of hot springs along the Jemez River. The lower group was owned by a man named Judt, the upper group by the Otero family.

"Each firm has erected comfortable bathing houses and sweating rooms," Reagan wrote. "The hotels have also been erected for the benefit of the health seekers. These springs are known throughout America and Europe; and it is not infrequent that one meets a foreigner here."

After the Oteros pulled out, a succession of owners ran the current Jemez Springs Bath House until 1943, when Dr. Bruington of Albuquerque gave the facility to the Order of the Servants of the Paraclete, affiliated with the Catholic Church. The structures and springs were used as a retreat for priests who came to the springs for a spiritual recharge. The hot springs remained in the hands of the church until 1961 when they were sold to the Village of Jemez Springs. The town still owns the springs and the bathhouse and leases out the operation of the springs.

The Jemez Springs Bath House was one of the original structures in the growing ranching community. It was built between 1870 and 1878 and was unusual in its stone-and-mud mortar construction and gabled roof. The original structure was expanded in 1940. On the grounds, an historic stone-and-log gazebo, built by the WPA in the 1930s, covers the main spring.

The current operators of the Bath House, Kate O'Donnell and Nina Crozier, have leased it since 1993. Because the building is on the register of New Mexico Historic Buildings, they followed suggestions from the state historian when they renovated the main structure. Their love of the building and their respect for the mineral water flowing into it will be obvious immediately to anyone visiting the Bath House.

Seven hot springs are located within the town of Jemez Springs. Three springs of interest are located near the Jemez Springs Bath House, and visitors should take a few minutes to walk behind the building before heading inside for a bath. Enclosed under the historic gazebo is Original Spring. It blasted into prominence in 1860 when the townspeople were shocked to

Built between 1870 and 1878 and expanded in 1940, the Jemez Springs Bath House is on the National Register of Historic Places.

find the spring erupting as a geyser. A nest of deposited minerals surrounds the vent, and the spring supports a species of algae that grows nowhere else. It is water from Original Spring that is used at the bathhouse.

Closer to the river is a turtle-backed mound of travertine stained with vertical streaks of algae. Steaming water spit from a perfect circle on top of the 2-foot-high mound completes the effect of a miniature volcano. A bit more to the south is Iron Spring, named for its red stain that once was thought to come from iron but is actually from algae.

Inside you'll find a homey atmosphere unmatched in the world of New Mexico's commercial mineral bathhouses. The staff is friendly and helpful, willing to go out of their way to make certain your stay is pleasant. The tastefully decorated bathing area is separated into men's and women's sections, each with four cement tubs. Privacy curtains separate the tubs, each of which has hot and

This historic gazebo, built by the Civilian Conservation Corps (CCC) in 1936, encloses Original Spring, which surprised town residents by erupting as a geyser in 1860.

cold faucets so you can adjust the temperature of the water to suit you. The quiet atmosphere is enhanced by gentle music. If you prefer an outdoor experience, a hot tub that holds up to six is located just outside. Suit and towel rentals are available.

A complete range of special services is offered. You can get a massage in one of the six special rooms or herbal wraps by licensed therapists. Facials, manicures, and pedicures are also available. A gift shop is in the main building.

The Jemez Springs Bath House is open year-round except Thanksgiving and Christmas, from 9 A.M. to 9 P.M. in summer and 10 A.M. to 7:30 P.M. in winter. The bathhouse and its special services are among the most popular spots in northern New Mexico, so you should always call ahead to make reservations. The modest fees are well worth the experience of soaking in the historic atmosphere.

The village of Jemez Springs—which proudly proclaims its selection as the 1995 All-American City—has limited services. However, the town offers a small convenience store, motel, several bed and breakfasts, and three restaurants. If you seek fancy surroundings, head south to Albuquerque, less than an hour's scenic drive away.

6. Bodhi Manda Zen Center Motel and Hot Spring

Location: the town of Jemez Springs
Type: privately owned primitive hot pools on the banks of the Jemez River
Services: A four-unit motel operated and located at the Zen Center. A short walk away from the simple restaurants and store in Jemez Springs.
Temperature: 95 to 110°F   **Discharge:** about 5 gpm
Elevation: 6,300 feet
Address: P.O. Box 8, Jemez Springs, NM 87025
Phone: (505) 829-3854

How to Get There: From Albuquerque, take Interstate 25 north to exit 242 and head west on New Mexico Highway 44. In 26 miles, at the town of San Ysidro, turn right onto New Mexico Highway 4. Continue 17 miles to the town of Jemez Springs. From Santa Fe, take US Highway 84/285 north about 15 miles to New Mexico Highway 502 toward Los Alamos. In 12 miles, bear right onto New Mexico Highway 4 and continue 55 miles to Jemez Springs.

Once in Jemez Springs, where the 25-mile-per-hour speed limit is strictly enforced, pass the town park and continue 0.1 miles. The Bodhi Zen Center is on the west side of the highway.

The Bodhi Manda Zen Center was established in 1973 to provide teaching in Zen Buddhism for all who wish to learn and practice it. Using water from one of the many vents within the town of Jemez Springs, the center has built a series of three primitive thermal pools that are available for use by motel guests.

Visitors can room at the four-unit motel that is part of the center, which entitles renters to use the hot pools on the grounds. Reservations are required to stay at the motel, which is closed Mondays and at various times throughout the year for special events. Always call ahead before planning a trip to these springs.

As is typical of the Jemez hot springs, water at more than 165 degrees flows from the springs and wells at the center. Each of the three pools is cooled to a different temperature, ranging from warm to very hot, allowing visitors to choose their ideal soaking water. You'll find the pools located a short walk from the motel, right along the Jemez River. The unsheltered, outdoor pools are more than 20 feet across and have a pebble bottom. Because of the exposed location, fall, winter, spring, and summer mornings and evenings are the best times to enjoy the waters. Bathers are required to wear swimsuits.

HOT SPRINGS OF THE UPPER RIO GRANDE BASIN

7. Manby Hot Springs

(*Also known as Stagecoach Hot Spring, Mamby Hot Spring,*
American Hot Spring)
Location: Rio Grande Wild and Scenic River Recreation Area, northwest
of Taos
Type: a primitive spring on the banks of the Rio Grande
Services: none. Nearest services are 10 miles away in Taos.
Temperature: 94 to 100°F **Discharge:** 30 gpm **Elevation:** 6,480 feet
Hike Rating: moderate, 1.5 miles round-trip
Maps: USGS Arroyo Hondo 7.5' quadrangle

Trailhead Access: From Taos, drive north on US Highway 64 to the
intersection with New Mexico Highway 522. Continue straight on New
Mexico Highway 522. In 5.3 miles, just before the road begins a long
descent, turn left on County Road B007. Continue 2.3 miles on this
gravel road, and turn left onto a very rutted dirt road. From this point,
a high-clearance vehicle or mountain bike is recommended. Follow the
main track, taking care to stay out of driveways along the way. After a
half-mile on the rutted track, take the left fork, then the right fork in
another 0.8 miles. Reach the parking area on the rim of the Rio Grande
Gorge at the unmarked trailhead in another half mile, 1.8 miles from
County Road B007. Note that the roads to the trailhead are impassable
during wet weather.

M anby Hot Springs offers the opportunity to soak in more than
just hot water. The springs and the route to them are steeped
in a rich natural and human history that begins with volcanoes
spewing 100-foot-thick walls of lava and ends, perhaps, with a

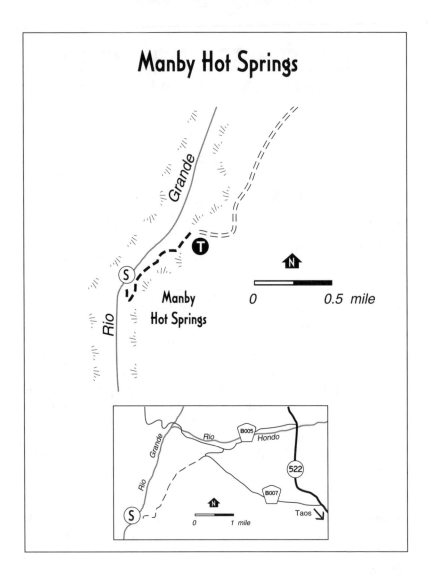

headless ghost haunting the springs on moonless nights. The trip to the springs guarantees a quality adventure, an interesting hike, and the chance to soak in a large spring while staring up at towering cliffs of stone rising up like the walls of a castle.

The story of Manby Hot Springs is a compressed view of the history of the state of New Mexico. The springs were used by the Pueblo people long before the Spanish sought to exploit its waters for the dream of perpetual youth. After a long, pastoral interlude, the final chapter involves an Anglo newcomer who attempted to create a real estate boom by conning the longtime residents out of their rights to the land.

Manby Hot Springs lies on the banks of the Rio Grande in the river's wild 90-mile gorge. The gorge is a narrow slice in the middle of a mountain-bounded depression called the Rio Grande rift. In the rift zone, the earth's crust is stretched thin, and hot magma lies relatively close to the surface. Fractures in the rock extend down to the magma. Groundwater circulates along the fractures, passing near enough to the magma to be heated and rise to the surface as hot water.

About 20 million years ago, lava pouring from dozens of nearby volcanoes filled the Rio Grande rift zone near Taos. Over the years, the Rio Grande carved a deep canyon through the hardened basalt. Black walls rise up from the river as much as 1,000 feet. Manby Hot Springs lies deep within the gorge in the most dramatic setting for a hot spring in the state.

Two ancient, geometric petroglyphs pecked into basalt boulders along the river demonstrate that the springs have been known for hundreds of years. Pueblo people from Taos or another village marked the location of the spring with their simple and mysterious rock art. Old Taos residents explain that one of the petroglyphs—three concentric circles with a solid dot in the middle—denotes the Pueblo name of the springs, *Wa-pu-mee.* This long-standing name, roughly translated as "water of long life," brought Spanish explorers to the area in the sixteenth century. The Europeans were searching for the Aztec's famed spring of perpetual youth, which was said to lie many days' journey north of Mexico City—a rather broad geographical range, but in the hopeful eyes of the Conquistadors, the description was a perfect fit for the Rio Grande Gorge. The Spanish found a well-worn trail from

Manby Hot Springs is on the banks of the Rio Grande in the river's wild 90-mile gorge.

the rim of the canyon to the hot springs, and undoubtedly their pulses quickened. Alas, their soak in the water failed to deliver the miracle for which they had come.

For many years, sheepherders and women from Taos and other small communities used the springs for washing clothes or bathing. In the 1890s, Taos merchants Albert Miller and Gerson Gusdorf widened the ancient trail to the springs into a road. They weren't interested in the springs, however, but in a commercial stage route to connect Taos with the nearest railroad station on the Denver and Rio Grande Railroad at Tres Piedras. A few yards downstream from the hot springs the merchants built a bridge across the river and cut switchbacks up the west wall of the gorge. They made money not only from stage service but also from collecting tolls for the use of the road and bridge. Eventually, the road brought a visitor who saw the hot springs as his own haven of peace and a potential source of wealth.

Arthur Rochford Manby, the black sheep of a wealthy English family, shipped off to the United States in 1890 to make his own fortune. He drifted into Taos and got involved in several mining schemes that all failed. Turning from mining, Manby saw his opportunity for riches in the convoluted legal battles involving Spanish land grants in northern New Mexico. With little capital, he quietly bought up dozens of small farms on the Antonio Martinez Land Grant; then, on the basis of a legal technicality, he boldly laid claim to the entire 66,000-acre grant.

The western boundary of the grant reached to the Rio Grande, and Manby assumed possession of the hot springs. Around 1906, Manby cleared out the largest pool and built a crude plank hut over it. He later replaced the hut with a fortress-like stone bathhouse. The door sat high on the windowless walls. Inside, Manby built a plank floor and a staircase leading down to the water. When Taos author Mabel Dodge Luhan first visited the bathhouse with her husband, he almost refused to enter the "very dark and sinister" house but came out an hour later feeling "all smoothed out."

Manby retreated to his bath to escape the pressure of his mounting debts. While soaking in his spring, he devised an elaborate scheme for developing the spring into a world-renowned resort. He had the water chemically analyzed and found it high in sodium and radon; he proclaimed the water possessed the power to cure nervousness, rheumatism, and intestinal troubles. Playing off the old Spanish theme of the spring of youth, he intimated that the Spanish were unaware that they had found the miracle spring. Manby pitched his plan for a hotel and private bathing chambers to wealthy easterners whom he lured over the rough road to the springs.

With legal battles still raging over ownership of the land, Manby couldn't scare up any investors to begin construction. After twenty years of scheming, Manby lost all his land holdings to his creditors. It turned out he never held title to the land where the hot springs lie. Bitter and paranoid, the old man hid in his house, coming out only at night to roam the streets of Taos. In July 1929,

Manby Hot Springs and the ruins of Manby's bathhouse.

Manby was found decapitated in his home, his large dog by his side. Whether Manby was murdered or died of natural causes and was later disfigured by his dog has never been determined.

The rugged nature of the Rio Grande Gorge usually makes access to the river an arduous adventure, but the old stagecoach road to Manby Hot Springs is the easiest of all the paths leading into the depths of the gorge. From the parking area on the rim, follow the wide but rocky road that angles into the canyon. The road soon narrows to a trail, offering spectacular views of the gorge and the river along the entire mile to the springs. It will take from twenty to thirty minutes to reach the springs. On the way down, watch for the retaining walls of the stagecoach road both adjacent to the path you are on and across the river as the abandoned road switchbacks up the other side. If you look carefully, you may see bubbles rising from a hot seep in the middle of the river.

The hot springs are just above the east bank of the river. Three rock-lined pools have comfortable sandy bottoms. The main pool, about 2 feet deep, is located against the west wall of Manby's bathhouse. It discharges about 30 gallons per minute and with a 20-foot diameter can hold up to ten bathers. Smaller, cooler pools are located closer to the river. These lower pools are submerged in the river during runoff, which usually lasts from late March to mid-May.

You'll find a variety of users at the springs, including local families, slope-weary skiers, out-of-state visitors, and nude sunbathers. This is one of New Mexico's most pristine hot pools. Please help keep the springs and the historical structures in the area free from trash and damage. Pack out everything you carry in. Do not enter Manby's bathhouse, as the walls are unstable. If you spot the nearby petroglyphs, don't touch them: Oils from your hands can damage the fragile desert varnish on the surface of the rocks.

The climb back to the rim on the gentle grades of the old stagecoach road ascends about 400 feet. It's an easy walk for those accustomed to the 6,000-foot elevation, but visitors from sea level should be prepared to take it slow. Also note that air temperatures in the gorge can soar over the century mark in summer. Spring and fall are the best times to enjoy the walk and the hot springs.

Plan on a leisurely half-day trip to visit the springs. Come prepared for more than the soaking. Explore the historic structures, watch for bald eagles soaring through the gorge and mergansers diving for fingerlings, or bring a fishing rod to enjoy some of the fine angling offered by the Rio Grande. You can explore upstream from the springs on a trail that follows the east bank, but the rocky Taos Box downstream is unsuitable for casual hikers.

The eclectic town of Taos offers visitors all the essential services, from groceries to regional specialty restaurants to a microbrewery. The community caters to a wide range of tastes, and everyone can find something pleasing. Nearby Taos Ski Area has a well-deserved reputation for excellent snow. In summer, rafting on the Rio Grande is a popular activity. Hiking or fishing in Carson National

Forest and the Wheeler Peak and Latir Wilderness Areas will provide the perfect prelude to a visit to the local hot springs. Camping is available in private campgrounds in Taos and along the Rio Hondo on the road to the ski area.

Whenever you drop in on the thermal waters along the Rio Grande, keep an eye out for Manby's ghost, searching for a bit of peace in the soothing waters of his spring.

8. Blackrock Hot Spring

(*Also known as Hondo Hot Spring*)
Location: Rio Grande Wild and Scenic River Recreation Area, northwest of Taos, west of Arroyo Hondo near the John Dunn Bridge
Type: a primitive spring on the banks of the Rio Grande
Services: none. Nearest services are 10 miles away in Taos.
Temperature: 98°F   **Discharge:** 0.5 gpm   **Elevation:** 6,540 feet
Hike Rating: easy, 0.5 miles round-trip
Maps: USGS Arroyo Hondo 7.5' quadrangle

Trailhead Access: From the Taos Plaza, go north on US Highway 64. Continue straight onto New Mexico 522 at the traffic signal where US Highway 64 turns left. Six miles past the intersection with US 64, just over a small bridge on the Rio Hondo, turn left onto the paved County Road B005. Drive slowly through the village of Arroyo Hondo. In 1 mile, the pavement ends. Cross another bridge and climb a short hill. Bear right in 0.1 miles and ignore the many side tracks as the main road snakes to the top of the hill before descending into the Rio Hondo Canyon. The road into the canyon is rough but passable by any vehicle. Cross the Rio Grande on John Dunn Bridge and continue 0.2 mile to the first hairpin turn and park off the road. Note that the road in Rio Hondo Canyon can be icy and hazardous in winter, and muddy and dangerous when wet.

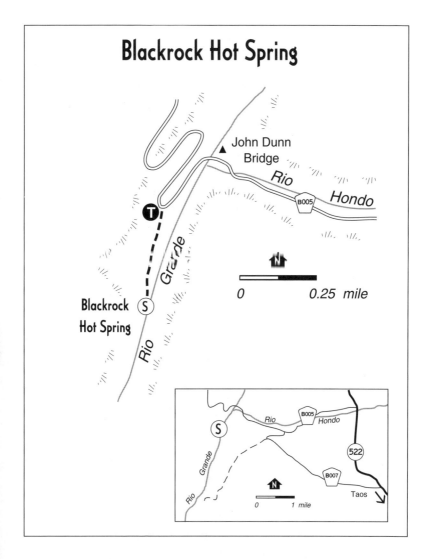

Blackrock Hot Spring

Few of northern New Mexico's bounty of hot springs have escaped the hands of developers and remain in a primitive condition. Blackrock Hot Spring has two characteristics that kept it from development: It has low flow, and it is located on the west bank of the rugged Rio Grande Gorge.

New Mexico is split roughly in half, north to south, by that great rent in the earth's crust, the Rio Grande rift. Tensional forces—somewhat related to the westward movement of the North American plate and its collision with the Pacific plate—are pulling New Mexico apart, creating an elongated, down-dropped block on the surface. Sediments washed down from the surrounding mountain ranges have partially filled the rift, and lava flowing on the surface from hundreds of faults bordering the rift has helped fill it too.

The Rio Grande has sliced a deep canyon through the great piles of lava in the northern portion of the rift zone. Ninety miles long and often almost 1,000 feet deep, the Rio Grande Gorge is a formidable barrier to travel across the northern third of New Mexico. With the major population center in the north located at Taos, over on the east side of the river, for the past thousand years, the west bank of the Rio Grande has remained isolated.

Construction of the Denver and Rio Grande Railroad from Colorado to Santa Fe on the plateau high on the west side of the Rio Grande provided plenty of stimulus to find a direct route from Taos to the trains. Two Taos merchants put up the first bridge across the river near Manby Hot Spring in the 1890s, and it wasn't long before a second, competing bridge was built a mile upstream at the mouth of the Rio Hondo.

In 1900, John Dunn of Taos purchased the bridge at the Rio Hondo with money he won at the poker table. It turned out that owning a bridge on the Rio Grande was quite a gamble, too, for the next spring flood took the bridge with it into the rugged gorge below. Dunn was a tireless man who quickly rebuilt the bridge and then expanded his business interests by starting a stage service running over the bridge from Taos to Sevilleta, a whistle stop on the railroad.

Said to be a fugitive from the Texas Rangers, Dunn was full of brilliant if somewhat shady ideas. He built a small hotel at his bridge and made the crossing an overnight stop on his stage line,

The trail to Blackrock Hot Spring in the spectacular Rio Grande Gorge.

an arrangement that forced passengers to pay for food and lodging before continuing to Taos the next morning. With the crossing securely his, Dunn eyed the hot springs a half-mile below, wondering how he could exploit them. He probably took a few guests over the rugged walking trail along the river to the springs, but the low flow of hot water, plus the fact that the springs were frequently covered by the runoff-swollen Rio Grande, kept Dunn from taking further advantage of the spring.

Far from isolated today, Blackrock Hot Spring is New Mexico's most accessible primitive mineral spring. From the parking area at the hairpin turn above Dunn's bridge, a well-developed trail dives from the road and heads downstream. The trail descends quickly to the river, reaching the spring in less than a quarter-mile.

The pool is small, and the volume of hot water is low. The mineral water issues from the base of the thick pile of black lava in a narrow drainage in the wall of the gorge. Boulders that have tumbled down the watercourse have completely covered the spot where the water bubbles up from the surface.

Despite its low volume, the flow from the hidden spring is collected in a deep, round pool about 12 feet in diameter that will comfortably hold five or six bathers. Soft sand has accumulated on the bottom, and there are rock ledges to sit on while enjoying the pool. Don't be deceived by the warm water temperatures in the top few inches of the pool: The deepest part of the pool can be considerably cooler. A lower pool sits at river level and is generally flooded during spring runoff in March, April, and early May. During peak runoff, the river may seep into the upper pool and chill its water to near-frigid.

Because of the beautiful canyon setting and its accessibility, Blackrock Hot Spring receives heavy use. If you are looking for privacy, head somewhere else. Also, thoughtless users have left unsightly trash scattered around the site. The locals are quite protective of this spring. Don't be a part of the problem: Remove all your trash, and visit this spring with a healthy dose of courtesy to other users.

Although Blackrock is a low-flow spring, the thermal pool is several feet deep.

9. Ojo Caliente Mineral Springs Spa

Location: northwest of Española, west of Taos along the Rio Ojo
    Caliente
Type: a developed resort with five distinctly different mineral springs
Services: mineral baths, swimming pool, bio-wraps, massage, and
    other body treatments; a hotel, restaurant, and gift shop are
    on the grounds. Other basic services are a short distance away
    in the town of Ojo Caliente.
Temperature: 99 to 113°F   **Discharge:** about 350 gpm total
Elevation: 6,310 feet
Address: P.O. Box 68, Ojo Caliente, NM 87549
Phone: (800) 222-9162
Web address: www.ojocalientespa.com

How to Get There: From Santa Fe, take US Highway 84/285 north
through Española. About 6 miles north of Española, turn right to stay
with US 285 as it splits off from US 84. Continue north about 16.5 miles
to the town of Ojo Caliente. Turn left onto New Mexico Highway 414,
which is just beyond the Ojo Caliente Post Office. Continue past the fire
station and over the Rio Ojo Caliente to the resort entrance. Turn left
and park in the large lot.

H ere's a chance for total relaxation, for allowing yourself to be
pampered. A refreshing change of pace from the many dusty
trails that lead to most of New Mexico's thermal water, the Ojo
Caliente Mineral Springs Spa offers a sublime contrast. It is a
resort that caters to your every whim and yet retains the rustic
charm that defines the haunting appeal of the state. A well-known
destination only an hour away from Santa Fe and Taos, the
springs, with its local flavor, probably attracts more visitors per
year than all other New Mexico hot springs combined.

Ojo Caliente boasts the state's only true mineral water hotel
and resort combination. In addition to a wide variety of baths and
special treatments to keep you feeling and looking good, Ojo

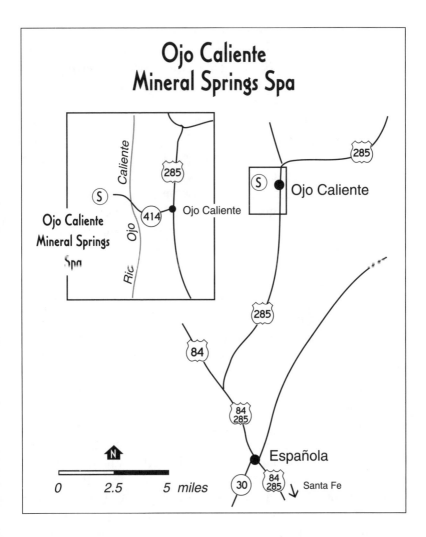

Ojo Caliente
Mineral Springs Spa

285

(S) Ojo Caliente

Ojo Caliente
Mineral Springs
Spa

Rio Ojo Caliente

285

(414) Ojo Caliente

(S)

285

84

84
285

N

0   2.5   5 miles

Española

30   84
      285   Santa Fe

offers a hotel and cottages, a café, outdoor swimming pools, horse-back rides, and a mountain bike trail. Although the spa caters to adults, it is a place the entire family can enjoy. In its own relaxed way, the place is jumpin'!

Like many other thermal features in the state, the five mineral springs along the Rio Ojo Caliente have been known since the time of the Anasazi. The mesas overlooking the valley hide the ruins of five extensive pueblos inhabited five hundred years ago by perhaps ten thousand people. The Tewa named the springs *P'soi*, "greenness water-issue," for the stains of algae that once dripped down the rocks.

Few springs have bubbled forth a well-worn legend in addition to soothing water. To the Tewa, the springs were the openings between the earth and the underworld, from which they believe people first emerged to the surface. The Tewa tell of the mythical hero Poseyemu, who came to life from piñon nuts gathered at the spring by a young virgin. The powerful chief made the pueblos prosper, then he disappeared into the East. It is said that he still visits his grandmother, who lives in the green waters of the springs, every five to seven years. The timing of his visits explains the cycle of piñon nut abundance.

Bathing in the mineral waters at Ojo Caliente was not only popular with the Pueblos but also with the Utes, Comanches, and Navajos who frequently visited the valley. Tradition has it that trails radiated out from the springs "like the spokes of a wheel." The tribes had a verbal agreement that a visitor from any group could soak in the waters in peace, even when the tribes were at war.

The nearby pueblo Posi-owinge was occupied when the Spanish first arrived at the springs but was abandoned early in the seventeenth century because of increasing raids by the Navajos. Spanish settlers were farming along the fertile valley of the Rio Ojo Caliente by the mid-1700s. It was a tough life on the frontier of Spain's colonies, and raids by the Utes and Comanches were common. Settlers who tried to leave the outpost were fined and imprisoned, but by 1778, the village was abandoned and the springs left to the Utes. When eighteen families sought to relocate at Ojo Caliente in 1790, the New Mexican governor insisted they build a sturdy fortress "since experience has proven that nobody can last there on account of its fatal position."

The village quickly gained some measure of stability; when Zebulon Pike passed through in 1805, he estimated that five hun-

*Just an hour away from Santa Fe, Ojo Caliente Mineral Springs Spa is the
state's only true mineral water hotel and resort combination.*

dred people lived there. Pike was impressed by the balmy climate
he found in Ojo Caliente in early March and by the *fandango* provided by the villagers. Of the springs, Pike said, "The greatest natural curiosity, the warm springs, which are two in number, about
10 yards apart and each afford sufficient water for a mill seat.
They appeared to be impregnated with copper, and were more
than 33 degrees above blood heat."

Lieutenant James Abert surveyed north-central New Mexico
just after the American conquest in 1846. Abert, too, was impressed by the springs and reported on their early therapeutic use.

> ". . . a village is built, called Ojo Caliente. The largest of
> these springs is 16 or 18 feet in diameter, and the water in
> the basin presents the appearance of boiling. . . . These
> waters have been recommended by Doctor Nagle, of Santa
> Fe, in many chronic diseases, and always with success."

The mineral springs were developed commercially in the 1860s by Antonio Joseph. A few bathhouses and a small hotel were built at the site, and three of the springs were widened and lined with rocks. By 1874, Joseph had as many as fifty guests at a time, most of them using the waters as a cure for rheumatism or syphilis. After the Denver and Rio Grande Railroad extended its tracks to Española in 1881, passengers could get off at Barranca station and travel by stage over the 10 bumpy miles to the springs. The main building, which today serves as the hotel, was built in 1917.

The Mauro family purchased the springs in 1932. Three generations of the family have run the resort with loving care and continue to do so today.

Since they were first chemically analyzed in the 1860s, the five major springs at Ojo Caliente have been known to exhibit very different mineral properties. The springs are touted as the only so-varied cluster of natural hot springs in the world. Hot water flows from the springs along a series of parallel fractures in the very ancient metamorphic rocks associated with the Tusas Mountains to the northwest. The heat source is unknown but may be related to the huge lava flows of Black Mesa, a 20-mile ridge that dominates the eastern skyline of the Ojo Caliente Valley.

Walking from the parking area to the bathhouses, visitors will immediately fall under the spell of Ojo. The grounds are pleasantly landscaped, the atmosphere is bright and cheerful, and everything is clean and well maintained. The buildings are a curious mix of old and new, from rambling adobes to the Spanish arches of the hotel to the new tin roofs of the refurbished bathhouses.

If you are visiting for the day, stroll over to the mineral bath office and pay the modest fee that will entitle you to use of the mineral pools for ninety minutes. Walk through the door into the courtyard where flowers bloom and shady benches beckon, along with the large mineral water swimming pool. The pool and the small tub behind it are open to all guests, including children. In summer, the pool is partly shaded by a colorful awning.

Within the adobe walls of the courtyard, you'll find the bathing complex. Two large bathhouses and changing areas offer showers, lockers, and a place to begin your stay. From there, you can explore the mineral pools.

Each developed spring is named for its dominant mineral constituent, and each is reputed to offer relief for different ailments. Near the bathhouses, water from the Lithia Spring is available for drinking. The water has trace amounts of lithium carbonate. Claims are made that lithium can help treat depression and relieves excess stomach gas.

Iron Spring contains a trace of that element, which gives a reddish tint to deposits from the 109-degree water. The proprietors point out that iron is known to be beneficial to the blood. Water from the spring is collected in a concrete-and-tile outdoor pool that will accommodate more than a dozen bathers. An attractive place to unwind is under the natural sandstone ledges of the cliffs behind the spa. To maintain a peaceful atmosphere, the Iron Pool is reserved for adults only.

Next to the Iron Pool is the Soda Pool, high in concentration of bicarbonate. This 10-foot-by-20-foot pool is partially enclosed, offering a secluded atmosphere. Pleasantly warm to soak in, the water from the spring is often used for drinking, especially by those with acidic stomach problems. Like the Iron Pool, Soda Pool is reserved for use by adults.

Many visitors feel that the mineral water from the 113-degree Arsenic Spring is the most therapeutic. The main pool near the main bathhouse is filled with this water. It is also circulated constantly into individual tubs within the bath houses, which may be rented for an additional fee. Trace amounts of arsenic are thought to help relieve arthritis and stomach ulcers.

The spa is open to visitors and hotel guests from 8 A.M. to 9 P.M. Sunday through Thursday and stays open to 10 P.M. on Friday and Saturday. Winter hours are a bit shorter.

What sets the Ojo Caliente Mineral Springs Spa apart from many of the other commercial springs in New Mexico is the wide variety of additional services that are offered. After a bath you can

A trace of iron gives a ruddy hue to the 109-degree water of Iron Spring.

enjoy a therapeutic massage, a facial, or a special body treatment such as the Salt Glow or Body Polish. Bio-wraps are particularly popular because of their relaxing qualities. You can get a seaweed, herbal, or Moor mud treatment; after which you'll be wrapped in layers of warm blankets. The price of the twenty-five-minute treatment includes twenty minutes in one of the private arsenic tubs. A wide variety of package deals means that everyone will find something to suit his or her interests. You can make reservations and pick up a handy appointment card, which doubles as your ticket for all special services, at the hotel office.

The historic hotel and its satellite cottages are the best way to enjoy more than a day at Ojo Caliente. The smallest rooms are in the hotel proper, with larger quarters, and slightly higher rates, found in the cottages. None of the rooms are equipped with showers or baths; all bathing is done in the bathhouses. The rooms are clean and well-cared-for. During the off-season from January to March and November to Christmas, rates are particularly attractive, but the lodging is reasonable any time of the year. A special discount is in effect for seniors. Included in the price of lodging is use of the mineral pools and two relaxation wraps. Whatever time of year you plan a visit, you'll want to make reservations.

The café offers casual dining, healthy food to complement the baths, and is open for breakfast, lunch, and dinner. The small village of Ojo Caliente offers additional restaurants and lodging possibilities, as well as gas and groceries.

Outdoor recreation is an important part of the Ojo Caliente experience. A great way to begin a day at Ojo Caliente is to take a two-hour horseback trail ride offered by nearby Round Barn Stables. Special archaeological horseback tours are also offered on weekends and in summer. If you want to provide your own power and get a good workout before relaxing in a pool, try the 6.5-mile mountain bike trail. You can bring your own bike or rent one on the grounds. It's a great little trail and offers several miles of winding single track.

The historic mineral baths at Ojo Caliente are one of the premier thermal water destinations in New Mexico. They deserve your attention either as a hotel guest or as a scenic day trip from a sightseeing or skiing visit to Santa Fe or Taos. You're bound to leave the quiet, shady haven on the banks of the Rio Ojo Caliente feeling more relaxed than ever.

10. Montezuma Hot Springs

Location: on the banks of the Rio Gallinas 6 miles west of Las Vegas, New Mexico
Type: a well-maintained, formerly commercial cluster of more than fifty springs on private property but open to the public
Services: none. Nearest services are 6 miles away in Las Vegas.
Temperature: 84 to 136°F   **Discharge:** 1 to 6 gpm
Elevation: 6,800 feet
Maps: USGS Montezuma 7.5' quadrangle

How to Get There: From Santa Fe, drive on Interstate 25 north about 60 miles to Las Vegas, New Mexico. Take the first Las Vegas exit, number 343, and turn left at the end of the off ramp. Go 0.4 miles and turn left onto New Mexico Highway 329, following the signs for United World College. In 2 miles, turn left onto New Mexico Highway 65. Continue 4.5 miles and bear left at the village of Montezuma, away from the direction of United World College. Park along the right side of the road 0.5 miles beyond Montezuma.

It is impossible to soak in the hot springs on the banks of the Rio Gallinas and not also enjoy the rich history of these springs. There's a sense of being watched by all the players in New Mexico's past—Pueblo people, Spanish settlers, American soldiers, railroaders, ranchers, and local townfolk. Much of the feeling comes from the scene to the north. On the hill overlooking the pools, the brown sandstone walls, towers, and gingerbread balconies of the

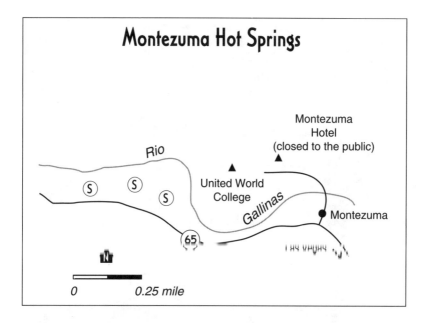

Montezuma Hot Springs

Montezuma
Hotel
(closed to the public)

Rio

United World
College

Gallinas

Montezuma

65

0   0.25 mile

Montezuma Hotel keep watch over the springs as they have for more than one hundred years. The hotel and the now-vanished bathhouses along the river once lured the rich and famous to mingle with the ranchers from the dusty town of Las Vegas. The Montezuma was the apex of nineteenth-century spa development in New Mexico.

The name Montezuma was first attached to the springs in 1846 when General Stephen Kearny's army rode into New Mexico. Kearny's men fell in with the Pecos Indians, who told the Americans a tale of the springs. According to the legend, Montezuma, the fabled Mexican emperor, was raised at the springs, far from Mexico, to learn patience, kindness, and nobility. When he was ready to ascend the throne, he was carried to Mexico by eagles, who brought him back to the springs each year to relax. Whether the Pecos were telling a solemn legend or pulling the Americans' legs will never be known, but the name stuck.

The hot springs at the foot of the Sangre de Cristo Mountains

Montezuma Hot Springs has a rich, colorful history as a mineral water attraction.

were used by the residents of Pecos Pueblo as early as the ninth century. Located at the boundary of the mountains and the Great Plains, the springs attracted Native American tribes who roamed the grasslands. After the founding of Las Vegas in 1821, the site was frequented by Spanish ranchers.

Twenty years later, William and Anthony Donaldson petitioned the Mexican government and obtained a land grant for the site of the hot springs; they erected the first commercial bathhouse at the site. By later standards, it was a simple affair, but it held six tubs for visitors.

When the Americans arrived in 1846, Lieutenant James Simpson scouted the terrain for General Kearny. Simpson detoured to the springs and gave the first scientific, quantified description of them. He also tried a little experiment.

"We put into the jagged cup or bowl of the fountain some eggs and raw venison, both of which were cooked in about twenty minutes," Simpson wrote in his report.

When Kearny moved on to Santa Fe, he left Colonel Edward Canby behind to locate a site for a hospital where convalescent soldiers could recover from their difficult journey over the Santa Fe Trail. Canby selected a bench near the springs for his hospital, reasoning that the mineral water would help speed the recovery of the sick. The army erected an adobe hospital building and several wood frame bathhouses. The site was so popular that many officers lobbied the brass to build Fort Union on the Rio Gallinas, and only the hospital's indefensible position in the narrow canyon prevented the move.

When the army pulled out of the Rio Gallinas Valley in 1862, Winfield Scott Moore bought that part of the property and converted the old hospital at the site into a small hotel. Moore succeeded in luring guests from the East to what he called Las Vegas Hot Springs and soon expanded his Abode Hotel. In 1879 the local newspaper reported that outlaw Jesse James—an old family friend of Moore—was "secretly" staying at the Adobe.

The meadow along the Rio Gallinas where the hot springs

flow isn't large, but soon the banks of the river were divvied up among at least three owners. A photograph from the late 1870s shows the meadow crisscrossed with white fences separating each property. The Adobe Hotel stood within its white border until fire destroyed it in 1881. Across the river, the Stone House sheltered guests and a pedestrian bridge linked the hotel to the bathhouse. But these were small-scale developments compared to what happened when railroad money was brought into the bustling little meadow above Las Vegas.

In 1878, as the Atchison, Topeka, and Santa Fe Railroad crossed Raton Pass and eased down the edge of the mountains toward Las Vegas and Santa Fe, an Arkansas developer familiar with the hot springs in his home state took note of the popularity of Moore's small resort. He found Moore unwilling to sell, but Frank Chapman, who owned a property adjacent to Moore's, was pleased to make a profit. When the first train chugged into Las Vegas a year later, the Arkansas man sold his hot spring property—purchased by Chapman in 1872 for eight thousand dollars—to a railroad syndicate for a cool one hundred and two thousand dollars.

The railroad men formed the Las Vegas Hot Springs Company and promptly erected a modest hotel and a two-story bathhouse. With promotions in the East and Europe and trains delivering passengers to Las Vegas, the response was overwhelming, so much so that when the first bathhouse was destroyed by fire after standing only six months, they immediately rebuilt it and made plans for a new, expanded hotel.

The new native granite bathhouse was designed to give five hundred baths a day. Thermal water was supplied by walling up twenty-three of the forty hot springs on the grounds and piping more than 30,000 gallons of mineral water a day. Separate men's and women's baths were located on the first floor. Above were a barber shop, hairdresser's, drugstore, and the resident doctor's office. In addition to mineral water tubs, vapor baths were offered, a combination of which cost seventy-five cents. The most popular

With the Stone Hotel in the foreground, the resort of Las Vegas Hot Springs stands in its heyday, circa 1898. (Courtesy of the Museum of New Mexico, neg. no. 76978.)

service was a thirty-minute mud bath where women took skin-care soaks in fresh mud thinned to the consistency of honey.

The first Montezuma Hotel was built to offer spa visitors more than a place to stay. From the start, it was designed to be a resort and a showplace. The fanciest furnishings were brought in from the East. With three stories, the hotel had 240 rooms. A massive power plant was built to provide steam for heat. Management was by Fred Harvey himself. To make it easier to get to the Montezuma, in 1882, the railroad built a spur line to the hot springs. The hotel was frequently filled with English guests seeking the mineral waters and a healthy climate.

Fire struck again on January 17, 1884, breaking out in the basement of the Montezuma and spreading throughout the hotel building. Undaunted, the Las Vegas Hot Springs Company rebuilt

The sprawling development of Las Vegas Hot Springs in the late nineteenth century. (Courtesy of the Museum of New Mexico, neg. no. 55393.)

the hotel—the second Montezuma—as a massive Queen Anne-style, brown sandstone structure perched on the hill overlooking the springs. No expense was spared: Billiard rooms, a bar, and a bowling alley were put in the basement; a white marble fountain dominated the lobby; and oak walls and floors gave a formal atmosphere to the dining room. The bathhouse was expanded to a thousand-bath-per-day capacity. In the hotel, a special water delivery system was added along with heat detectors to protect against fire. By October, the mineral spring business was again booming.

Incredibly, the hotel stood for barely six months before the now-familiar fire alarm was sounded yet again. Flames broke out on the fourth floor of the hotel and the hoses of the elaborate fire protection system were not long enough to reach the far end of the building to douse the flames—no one had bothered to measure them against the length of the hallways. The first two floors were saved, but the rest of the building was gone.

The owners decided to rebuild the top four floors on what was left of the hotel. They renamed the new hotel the Phoenix because, like the mythical firebird, it rose from the ashes of the former structure. The name never had widespread use, however, and nearly everyone still called it the Montezuma.

The Phoenix opened in 1886 with only sixty guests. The resort was already feeling the effects of the expanding tourist industry in the Southwest. Resorts such as the La Fonda in Santa Fe, Manitou Springs in Colorado, and El Tovar at the Grand Canyon took visitors away from the springs at Montezuma. In 1893, the Las Vegas Hot Springs Company ceased operation of the hotel.

A succession of lessors and owners used the hotel and springs for weekend dances, as a retreat for priests, and as colleges. Eventually the hotel and hot springs came into the hands of the Armand Hammer Foundation, which operates a branch of the United World College on the grounds today.

The hot springs, located on land owned by the United World College, are open to the public through the generosity of the owners. A few sensible restrictions are placed on the use of the springs. The pools are open from 5 A.M. to midnight, and campus security along with county and state police enforce the hours. No alcohol is permitted on the grounds, and the use of soap or herbal additives in the water is prohibited. Bathing suits are required. Visitors are requested to keep noise levels low.

From the parking area along Highway 65, a sign points the way to the springs. Three gates in the fence along the road provide access into the area. All the springs are found in a meadow along the Rio Gallinas. Hot water seeps from the ground in more than forty spots, some of which are still rock-lined from the original development of the bathhouse in the early 1880s. The ground around the springs is soggy, wet, and warm. A thick mat of white-flowered yerba mansa carpets the low-lying areas, and in late summer, scarlet cardinal flowers light up the meadow.

You'll find six to eight rock-and-concrete tubs open for soaking. Most are small, suitable for one or two people, but a few hold eight to ten bathers. The older pools, up to 3.5-feet deep, are not very attractive. Three newer pools near the east end of the springs

These attractive pools at Montezuma Hot Springs were built by volunteers.

are more comfortable and not as deep. A tiered set of three pools at the west end is a sheer delight and offers the hottest water. The pools are a most pleasant temperature, ranging from 95 to 110 degrees.

Gravel pathways link the pools. The smaller pools take a bit of abuse and a few have a low-flow rate and quite a growth of algae—you would do well to stay out of these. Stroll around the grounds for a few minutes and find a pool that strikes your fancy.

No services are available at Montezuma, but Las Vegas, 6 miles down the road, has lodging, restaurants, gas, groceries, and other supplies. If you are looking for accommodations in the area, give the Las Vegas Chamber of Commerce a call at (505) 425-8631.

Whenever you visit the pools, remember that the area is on private land and can be closed to the public at any time. Treat this small haven with plenty of respect: Follow the rules set by the landowner, take all your trash with you, and don't throw anything in the pools. The area is maintained by volunteers and remains a wonderful place for a mineral bath solely because of their efforts.

HOT SPRINGS OF THE LOWER RIO GRANDE BASIN: TRUTH OR CONSEQUENCES

A Brief History of the Area

Below the rounded hump of Turtleback Mountain are hot springs that rank among the most voluminous in the world. Indeed, the 2.5 million gallons of hot water per day that pour from the ground along the banks of the Rio Grande have given rise to New Mexico's most extensively developed mineral water area.

Artifacts found in the sand surrounding the hot springs indicate that members of the Mimbres culture visited the thermal features more than eight hundred years ago. More recently, the Apaches came to the springs to use the warm mud as a salve for healing their wounds. The guerrilla warrior Geronimo reputedly called the springs along the Rio Grande his favorite, a legend that has given the most prominent vent in the area the name Geronimo Springs.

El Camino Real, the main Spanish and Mexican road from Mexico to Santa Fe in the eighteenth century, passed close to the springs. According to legend, the hot water was unnoticed by Spanish travelers until a friendly Native American revealed its secret location under a huge, flat removable rock.

A Spanish mission was established at Palomas Ojo Caliente, "Hot Spring of the Doves," to protect and give shelter to freighters hauling precious metal from the mines at Santa Rita to the west. When the Rio Grande was swollen with runoff, the teamsters were forced to wait perhaps for weeks before they could cross the river to continue down the Camino Real on the east bank. They didn't seem to mind the delay, which gave them ample opportunity to soak in the mineral water.

In more recent times, Fort McRae was established on the banks of the Rio Grande in 1864, and soldiers from the fort often came to bathe in the hot springs. When the post was abandoned in 1884, the Sierra County commission appropriated four hundred dollars to build a shelter over the spring named for Geronimo. Because of the remote location, only area ranchers used the springs, which remained little more than sandy-bottomed, rock-lined pools that overflowed into the Rio Grande. As more settlers moved into the area, two cement pools were built on the site. Other springs in the area were claimed by the John Cross Cattle Company, which erected a bathhouse over one spring to give its cowboys a retreat from the rigors of the range.

In 1911, construction began on Elephant Butte Dam, and the geothermal area soon became the center of a small town, Palomas Hot Springs. The new community served as a supply center for the construction site, while most workers lived at the dam site. Because it was a federal construction project, alcohol was not allowed in the residential area. To compensate for this shortcoming, Palomas Hot Springs soon acquired a disproportionate number of bars and dance halls. When the dam was completed in 1916, many workers moved to Hot Springs (the town dropped "Palomas" from its name), and a caravan of buildings from the construction site was sectioned, trucked, and reassembled in the growing town.

Construction of Elephant Butte Reservoir brought roads and recreational opportunities to Hot Springs, and the town quickly gained a reputation as a vacation center. With increasing automobile traffic in the 1930s, many entrepreneurs began to develop spas from the local hot springs. Hotels and apartments, as well as a community center, offered mineral baths to residents and visitors. Even the state of New Mexico got into the act by constructing a State Bathhouse. By 1935, Hot Springs was one of the state's largest resort cities.

From 1914 to 1951, the quiet village on Elephant Butte Reservoir was known as Hot Springs. The name was an old one, a variation of the early Spanish name *Ojo de Zoquete*, "mud spring."

This postcard, circa 1920, of the now-defunct James Mineral Baths in downtown T or C proclaims: "One of the Modern Bath Houses in Hot Springs, N.M." (Photo by C. Phillips; courtesy of the Sierra County Historical Society.)

The traditional name was to change shortly after Ralph Edwards and the staff of the popular radio show "Truth or Consequences" laid plans to celebrate the show's tenth anniversary. Edwards searched for a town willing to change its name to that of his program. New Mexico State Senator Burton Roach of Hot Springs got wind of the scheme and thought it a grand way to give the little resort town some national publicity. It also would help eliminate the problem with the name "Hot Springs," which was shared with more than seventy other towns around the nation. The name change was put to a vote, and the townspeople favored the change four to one. Edwards and the entire radio crew came to town in late March 1950 and on April 1, they broadcast their tenth-anniversary show from the high school auditorium of the newly christened town of Truth or Consequences—T or C for short.

The name remains controversial—almost any lengthy conversation with a resident will eventually turn to the change—but in three attempts to return the name to Hot Springs, citizens have overwhelmingly voted to keep the new name.

The geology of the thermal waters of the T or C area has long been studied. Along the southern portion of the Rio Grande rift, deep circulation of groundwater provides the heat to push the 98- to 114-degree water to the surface. The heated water moves through a surprisingly small set of fractures in the underlying rock, spilling out onto the surface in a confined band only a quarter-mile long. The small area of discharge makes it easy to guess the water's path through the subsurface. Deep underground, thermal water moves through cavities and along fractures in the Magdalena limestone. When the moving water reaches the fault zone that marks the upper limit of the limestone, it travels along the tilt of the rock. Surface gravels over the limestone act as a barrier, and the water flows out onto the surface along the contact. Before the extensive development of the springs, hot water flowed from the discharge point into the Rio Grande, raising by several degrees the temperature of the river downstream.

The temperature, volume, and chemical makeup of the springs remain remarkably constant. Every day more than 2.5 million gallons of sodium-potassium-chloride-rich water issues from the springs. The chemical composition of the thermal water is completely different from that of the nonthermal water pumped from wells in the T or C area, evidence that the two come from entirely different sources.

T or C remains primarily a ranching and mining supply center, not surprising when you consider the lack of support for the old name of Hot Springs. The heritage of the health and recreation boom of the 1930s is obvious throughout town. It was— and remains—a resort town for the unpretentious. You won't find fancy spas, high-class talk, or expensive lodging in T or C, just the basics that will get you into the mineral waters quickly and comfortably.

The Geronimo Springs Museum on Main Street is a quaint introduction to the history of the area. Like all intriguing local historical museums, this one is a delightful hodge-podge of unrelated facts that reveals as much about the history of Sierra County in the style of telling as in the story itself. It's worth an hour of your time to take in the eclectic collection of artifacts on display that includes mastodon skulls, Apache history, geology of the mines and thermal waters, and an incredible assortment of Southwest Indian pottery.

The entire lower downtown section of T or C sits just above the sheet of thermal water making its way to the nearby Rio Grande. You won't find any bubbling springs or undeveloped natural pools within the town limits. Each thermal water establishment has its own way of bringing together the warm underground flow and the people who seek it. You'll notice that each bathhouse touts water temperatures between 98 and 112 degrees. Water temperatures throughout the thermal area vary with the amount of water flowing in the Rio Grande, which in turn is regulated by irrigation requirements. Water temperatures are on the cool side of the range from late summer through winter.

While the town once boasted more than a dozen bathhouses, the number has fallen to six, and it's an adventure to explore them all. Restaurants and lodging are available in town, as are many RV parks. You'll find all the supplies you need in town, including groceries, gas, fast food, and major chain hotels. Tent campers would do well to look outside the town for a campground. Nearby Elephant Butte State Park offers plenty of lakeside sites complete with cool evening breezes.

The town of Truth or Consequences is located just off Interstate 25 about 72 miles south of Socorro, 150 miles south of Albuquerque, and about 80 miles north of Las Cruces. From the north, take the T or C exit, which will lead in 2 miles to Main Street. The southern approach is via the New Mexico Highway 51 exit from the Interstate, which leads in 4 miles to Broadway.

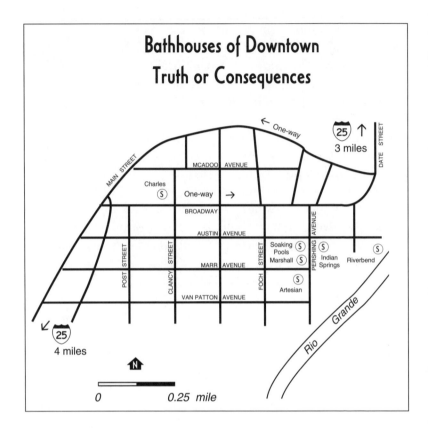

Bathhouses of Downtown Truth or Consequences

11. Indian Springs Bath House

Type: privately owned bathhouse with attached lodging
Services: large mineral bath with natural flow
Temperature: 106°F
Address: 218 Austin Avenue, Truth or Consequences, NM 87901
Phone: (505) 894-2018
Rates: by the half-hour, very reasonable; free baths with room

How to Get There: Heading east on Broadway in downtown Truth or Consequences, turn right onto Pershing Avenue. Go one block south to

Indian Springs Bath House offers a unique setting and lots of privacy.

Austin Avenue. Cross Austin and enter the Indian Springs Bath House parking area on the left.

A one-pool bathhouse: Don't let the appearance of Indian Springs fool you. If you want a private, relaxing soak, especially in the presence of someone whose company you enjoy, the small, partially underground bathhouse is one of the best in town.

Indian Springs boasts the only naturally flowing mineral bath in town. The owners have taken advantage of their location right on the "Hot Ditch" that flows through downtown T or C by digging a pool into the shallow water table. Water seeps into the gravel-and-sand-bottomed hole without the aid of pumps, maintaining a constant through current.

This bath is surprisingly comfortable. Enclosed in a cedar plank shack about 20 feet by 10 feet, the subterranean pool invites lingering baths. The interior is functional, with no fancy frills, and the water is always a perfect temperature.

The bathhouse is open from 7 A.M. to 11 P.M. daily. It is uncrowded during the day and in the summer, but reservations are recommended for evening hours and throughout the week in winter. You can soak in the pool for a half-hour at a time for a most reasonable fee, and before and after be entertained by the hostess, whose crusty view of life and her adopted town is as refreshing as the waters.

If you are only interested in easy access to the bath, you might consider a stay in the attached room, but the accommodations are small and the bare-bones style may not suit all tastes.

12. Charles Motel and Bath House

Type: privately owned bathhouse with attached lodging
Services: men's and women's bathhouses, massage, reflexology
Temperature: 98 to 112°F
Address: 601 Broadway, Truth or Consequences, NM 87901
Phone: (505) 894-7154
Rates: baths by the hour, reasonable; rooms from daily to monthly, very reasonable

How to Get There: The Charles is located at the corner of Clancy Street and Broadway in downtown T or C.

Built during the health-boom years of the 1930s by developer Charles Lockhart, the Charles Motel and Bath House wears its age well. One of the best maintained and managed bathhouses in town, the Charles shows ample signs of the loving care given by previous owner Bonnie Hille and current owner Kathy Clark. From the pleasantly landscaped ground to the inviting lobby to the sparkling baths themselves, the Charles will please all visitors.

The bathhouse is divided into men's and women's sides, but special arrangements can be made for couples looking to enjoy

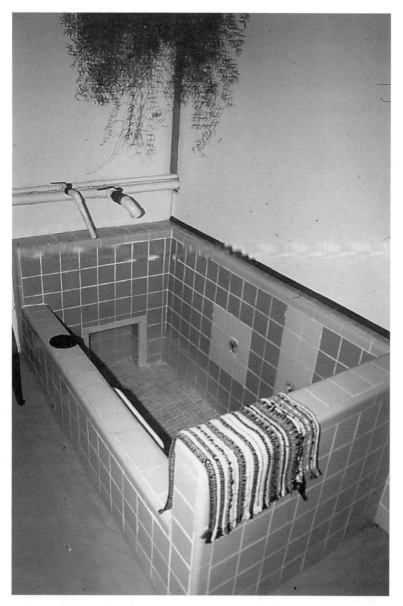

The luxurious ceramic tubs at Charles Motel and Bath House feature reclined tile bottoms for comfort.

the waters together. There are a total of nine tubs, separated from the others by floor-length dividers. The ceramic tubs are large and luxurious, with reclined tile bottoms for maximum comfort. Arrangements can be made for a family to use one of the bath facilities. Hot mineral water is piped into each bath from the Charles's thermal well, and a cold water tap permits bathers to regulate the bath temperature.

The fact that there are nine tubs means you'll rarely have to wait for a soak. If you are looking for a mineral bath on the spur of the moment, the Charles is often your best bet in T or C. The bathhouse is open from 8 A.M. to 9 P.M. seven days a week. The tubs rent by the bath; shower and sauna facilities are available.

The pleasing, well-apportioned rooms of the motel (one- or two-bedroom kitchenettes) are available for reasonable daily, weekly, or monthly rates. These are some of the nicest rooms in town, and they are only a few steps from the bathhouse. The friendly staff can arrange not only mineral baths but massage, reflexology, and other forms of healing therapy.

If you're on a tight schedule and are looking for a high-quality mineral bath, stop at the Charles.

13. Artesian Bath House and RV Park

Type: privately owned bathhouse with attached RV park
Services: bathhouse
Temperature: 98 to 108°F
Address: 312 Marr, Truth or Consequences, NM 87901
Phone: (505) 894-2684
Rates: baths by the hour, very reasonable; RV space daily, weekly, or monthly, very reasonable

How To Get There: The Artesian is located at the corner of Marr and Pershing Avenues, south of Broadway.

Downtown Truth or Consequences is teeming with underlaying thermal water.

True to its name, the Artesian gets its constant flow of hot mineral water via the last remaining artesian well from the deep drillings of the 1930s. Although it varies slightly with local hydrologic pressure, at least 70 gallons per minute flow from the well, ready for use by bathers.

Five single-sized and three double-to-family-sized baths are rented by the hour at very reasonable rates. A special rate is offered for seniors, a discount not common in T or C. The double tubs run a bit more than the singles, but they are still a good deal. The bathhouse is open from 8 A.M. to 6 P.M. and is closed on Wednesdays.

Each private bathing room includes a comfortable bench and a large ceramic tub. Mineral water at a neutral pH of 7 is run into the tubs, and a cold shower is also provided. The use of biodegradable soap and shampoo is permitted. A nominal fee is charged for towel rental. Massage is available by appointment.

You can stay nearby by taking a space at the attached RV park.

The sites on the gravel lot have hookups and are reasonably priced.

14. Riverbend Hot Springs

Type: privately owned lodging affiliated with Hosteling International offering mineral baths
Services: mineral water baths
Temperature: 98 to 108°F
Address: 100 Austin, Truth or Consequences, NM 87901
Phone: (505) 894-6183
Rates: baths by the hour, moderate

How To Get There: Heading east on Broadway in downtown Truth or Consequences, turn right onto Pershing Avenue. Go south one block to Austin Avenue. Turn left and continue on Austin until the road dead ends at Riverbend Hot Springs.

Slip into the warm water tubs at Riverbend, and you'll almost imagine you've hiked into a primitive spring. Boasting T or C's only outdoor, open-air mineral bath, Riverbend offers a striking view of Turtleback Mountain from its perch on the banks of the Rio Grande. As the river flows peacefully by, bathers can feel the tightness of their muscles flowing away with the river. Riverbend is the most alluring soak in T or C, and it definitely caters to a younger crowd. The spring is affiliated with Hosteling International but offers mineral baths to the public.

Three small tubs sit under a shady awning. The three have been created from a 20-foot-by-5-foot fishing bait tank, providing the tubs with the name "Hot Minnow Baths." Each tub is at a slightly different temperature than its neighbors. They are drained twice a day to eliminate the need for chemical treatment. Guests can use the baths at any time, and nonguests can come by between 10 A.M. and 10 P.M.

Although you can soak and watch ducks cruising the course

of the river or hawks soaring over the nearby desert, there's a social atmosphere to the tubs. Their public nature requires that bathers wear suits. Visit during the day for a bit of peace, for in the evening the bathing deck can get crowded.

15. Marshall Miracle Hot Springs

Type: privately owned bathhouse
Services: baths in a relaxing atmosphere
Temperature: 103 to 108°F
Address: 311 Marr, Truth or Consequences, NM 87901
Phone: (505) 894-9286
Rates: baths by the hour, very reasonable

How To Get There: Reach the Marshall by heading east on Broadway to Pershing Avenue. Turn right and continue two blocks to the colorful buildings of this mineral bathhouse.

M arshall Miracle Hot Springs caters to traditional soakers and those seeking a more spiritual bent to their mineral bath. The current owners can supply several extras—music, incense, and more—that will turn your bath into a completely relaxing experience.

Three private 6-foot-square-by-4-foot-deep pools offer unique baths. Supplied by a constant flow-through of water ranging from 104 to 108 degrees, these gravel-bottomed concrete pools offer the chance for a deep soak. The walls are colorfully decorated with replicas of Mimbres designs. Benches border the pools and provide comfortable seating.

Reasonable rates for hour or half-hour baths are charged. Because of the limited number of pools, reservations are highly recommended, particularly in winter and on weekends.

If you are looking for a place to unleash your inner self, look into the mineral baths at the Marshall.

Marshall Miracle Hot Springs caters to those seeking a spiritual experience from their baths.

16. Hot Springs Soaking Pools

Type: privately owned bathhouse
Services: baths, showers, and massage
Temperature: 104 to 108°F
Address: 300 Austin Avenue, Truth or Consequences, NM 87901
Phone: (505) 894-2228
Rates: soaks by the half-hour, reasonable

How To Get There: Reach Hot Springs Soaking Pools by heading east on Broadway to Pershing Avenue and turning right. Continue one block to Austin Avenue and the bathhouse is located on the right.

An historic bathhouse located right on the "Hot Ditch," the Hot Springs Soaking Pools offers individual, couples, or families a pleasant bathhouse experience with high-quality mineral water. The mud baths of the Spanish days were located here, but today you'll find only clean, hot water being used.

Soaking Pools is the oldest continuously operating bathhouse in T or C.

The Soaking Pools is the oldest continuously operating bathhouse in T or C. The building was constructed in the original flurry of activity in the 1930s. It was remodeled in the 1970s by Karl and Ceil Kortemeier, and more recently by their son, who now manages the bathhouse.

The bathhouse offers three individual tubs and two larger family "pools." Each pool is fed by its own source of mineral water, and each has a natural flow of about 40 gpm, among the largest flow-throughs in the area. The pools have pleasing gravel bottoms, and the springs bring up a small amount of silt with the water. The bathhouse is bright and attractive, featuring stained-glass partitions between the pools.

The pools can be rented by the half-hour and may be reserved outside normal operating hours. The bathhouse is open Monday, Tuesday, Thursday, and Friday afternoons, 9 A.M. to noon and 3 P.M. to 7 P.M. on Saturday; and Sunday from noon to 7 P.M. Closed Wednesdays. It's best to call in advance for a reservation.

HOT SPRINGS OF THE GILA RIVER BASIN

17. Melanie Hot Spring

Location: northwest of Silver City, 3 miles south of Gila Hot Springs
Type: a primitive hot spring along the east bank of the Gila River
Services: none. Gas and groceries are available in Gila Hot Springs, 2
     miles north of the trailhead; other services are 38 miles away
     in Silver City.
Temperature: 112°F
Discharge: 20 gpm
Elevation: 5,520 feet
Hike Rating: easy, 4 miles round-trip
Maps: USGS Gila Hot Springs 7.5' quadrangle, identified as Spring
     (Hot)

Trailhead Access: From the intersection of US Highway 180 and New
Mexico Highway 15 (Pinos Altos Road) in Silver City, take New Mexico
Highway 15 north toward Gila Cliff Dwellings National Monument.
Travel is slow on this narrow, winding road, and it will take at least an
hour and a half to drive 37.5 miles to the Gila River Trailhead. The trailhead is located 0.1 miles east of the Upper Gila River Bridge near a
primitive camping area. Turn right onto the gravel access road, then
continue straight to the parking area at the confluence of the East and
West Forks of the Gila River.

The Gila Wilderness is a sprawling roadless area of high desert
grasslands, lush canyons, and forested mountains that encom-
passes more than 1,000 square miles. The largest in New Mexico,
the wilderness holds one of the nation's most complex network of
trails, an endless delight for hikers, backpackers, and horseback

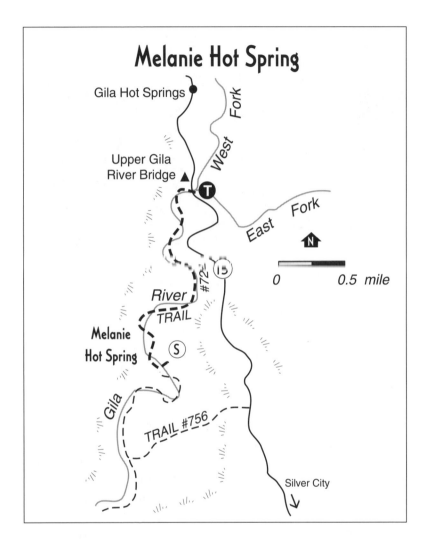

Melanie Hot Spring

Gila Hot Springs

West Fork

Upper Gila
River Bridge ▲

T

East Fork

N

0   0.5 mile

15

#72

River
TRAIL

Melanie
Hot Spring

S

Gila

TRAIL #756

Silver City

riders. The hot springs hidden in these empty acres offer the finest
backcountry thermal water experiences in the Southwest.

Serving with the Forest Service in the Gila in 1916 was young
Aldo Leopold, one of the early trail riders. The ranger was so
taken by the Gila that he developed the concept of wilderness to
insure that places like the Gila would remain untouched for future

Near Melanie Hot Spring, the canyon of the Gila River is 800 feet deep.

generations. I, for one, am thankful for Leopold's foresight, and if you make the effort required to reach any of the Gila's thermal waters, you'll be thankful too.

Although it receives more visitors on a spring weekend than Leopold saw in a year, the Gila hasn't changed much since it was proclaimed the nation's first wilderness area in 1924. The wide open desert hills, dry pine forest, and contrasting lush canyon bottoms are a landscape of stark beauty, but one that, through the miracle of snowmelt and rainfall flowing down from the highest peaks, remains approachable. The sun-burned slopes are adorned in unusual cacti, yuccas, and agave, where only a few yards away, you can find the soothing shade of an Arizona sycamore. Exotic mammals like the collared peccary, ringtail, and coatimundi roam through the thin cloak of vegetation. As part of New Mexico's constellation of enchantment, the Gila is one of the brightest stars.

From the geologist's standpoint, the Gila is a huge pile of volcanic rock where about 40 cubic miles of magma have been extruded from the earth. The eruptions began about 50 million years ago and continued for 30 million years. The mounds of lava are thousands of feet thick and are often eroded into cliffs that tower over the rivers like fortress walls. Most impressive is the Moonstone tuff—laid down as hot-ash flow raced at 200 miles per hour down the flanks of vanished volcanoes—which forms 700-foot columns along the canyons of the West and Middle Forks of the Gila River. The buff and orange cliffs create a backdrop of towering pillars on scenic hikes through these canyons.

A northwest-trending belt of hot springs runs from the ranch settlement of Gila Hot Springs to the plains of the Meadows, through the heart of the Gila Wilderness. The springs lie on the edges of a huge down-dropped block of surface roughly 5 miles wide and 20 miles long. Water circulates deep underground, in heated by the earth's interior, then finds its way to the surface along the faults bordering the sinking block. The result is New Mexico's highest concentration of thermal water.

At the southern end of the chain of springs, Melanie Hot Spring isn't very far from the road, it only seems that way. Once you enter the 40-mile-long canyon of the Gila River and begin the 2-mile walk to the spring, the rest of the world melts away behind towering cliffs and even taller mountain slopes. This thermal area lacks the deep pools that attract visitors to other Gila Wilderness springs; however, it does have a picturesque setting, and the grand scenery of the Gila Canyon alone makes the short hike worthwhile. If you are looking for solitude, scenery, and a chance to soak your feet or take a dip in a warm river, Melanie Hot Spring is for you.

No one seems to know the Melanie who gave the spring its name, but locals tell the story of one old-timer who was determined to get a decent hot bath out of the spring. Because the hot water issues from a vent on a steep slope, there is little room to build a collecting pool. Before the expansion of the Gila Wilderness, this gentleman waterproofed a small flatbed trailer and hauled it down the then-open road that paralleled the river. He maneuvered the trailer into the river, secured it with rocks, and caught the drips from the spring before they hit the river, creating an open-air hot tub.

The route to the spring requires crossing the Gila River ten times. As a result, Melanie Hot Spring can be reached only when the Gila River is running low and when the water temperatures are warm enough for comfortable wading. In general, spring run-off occurs from mid-March through early to mid-May. However, depending on winter snowpack and spring temperatures, these dates can be pushed several weeks earlier or later. Water temperatures drop to uncomfortable levels by late October. Consider a trip to Melanie Hot Spring from mid-May through mid-October. Whenever you make the trip, take along the proper equipment and plan to hike in comfortable wading shoes. You can wear an old pair of running shoes or sturdy all-terrain sandals. It's also a good idea to call the Gila Wilderness Ranger District ([505] 536-2250) for the latest river conditions.

Note that you can also reach Melanie Hot Spring via the rugged and steep Alum Mountain Trail (#756). From the well-marked trailhead along New Mexico Highway 15, this route drops 1,500 feet to the river in a little less than 2 miles. The sun-blasted slope makes for a hot hike, especially on the way out. Except in late fall, hikers should use the river trail to reach the spring.

The wet route to the spring follows the Gila River Trail 724 on the floodplain of the river. From the trailhead at the confluence of the East and West Forks of the Gila, immediately cross the main stem of the Gila and head downstream under the highway bridge. Follow the gravel road on the west bank for 200 yards, then again cross the river. The wide, sandy trail soon enters the Gila Wilderness, passing on wide sand-and-gravel bars under black cliffs that drop straight to the river. In summer, sections of the trail can be hot, but there's plenty of shade at intervals under spreading cottonwoods. At times the trail is ill defined, but the river and cliffs will lead you on the natural course downstream.

After walking downstream about 2 miles, you will cross the river for the ninth time. (Don't count crossings of narrow side

Flow from Melanie Hot Spring drips into the Gila River.

channels.) Stay close to the river and watch and listen. Just downstream from the crossing, the river turns a hard right at a dramatic rhyolite cliff. Immediately downstream, you will hear trickles of water and see colorful bands of algae drooping into the Gila. Find a suitable place to cross the river once again, heading for narrow shelves of rock below the spring.

A grassy patch 25 feet above the river locates the hot spring. You can climb to the spring and soak your feet in a small grotto where warm water drips from the rocks, or try the one-person soaking puddle that doesn't seem to hold enough water. Most visitors soak in the river itself at the point where the warm water from the spring drips into small but deep pools.

The broad flats in the canyon bottom both above and below offer a variety of shady campsites for those who wish to spend the night in the wilderness. You can also spend the night in the primitive camping areas located along the East and West Forks near the trailhead, or a couple of miles up the road in Gila Hot Springs.

18. Lightfeather Hot Spring

(*Also known as Middle Fork Hot Spring*)
Location: 42 miles northwest of Silver City, one-half mile north of the Gila Visitor Center
Type: a primitive hot spring along the Gila River
Services: Basic services are available at Gila Hot Springs, 3 miles east; other services are 42 miles away in Silver City
Temperature: 130°F   **Discharge:** 47 gpm   **Elevation:** 5,620 feet
Hike Rating: easy, 1 mile round-trip
Maps: USGS Gila Hot Springs 7.5' quadrangle

Trailhead Access: From the intersection of US Highway 180 and New Mexico Highway 15 (Pinos Altos Road) in Silver City, take New Mexico Highway 15 north toward Gila Cliff Dwellings National Monument. Travel is slow on this narrow, winding road and it will take at least an

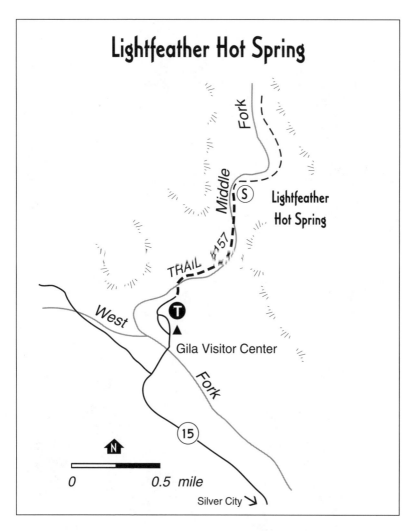

Lightfeather Hot Spring

Fork

Middle

TRAIL #157

(S) Lightfeather
Hot Spring

West

T
▲

Gila Visitor Center

Fork

(15)

N

0   0.5 *mile*

Silver City ↘

hour and a half to drive 42 miles to the Gila Visitor Center. Park in the
backcountry parking area located behind the center.

The Apache child *Goyahkla*—One Who Yawns—was born
around 1825 at the spot the tribe called No-doyon Canyon. As
an old man, then known to all as Geronimo, the Apache chief

Was this the birthplace of the feared Apache warrior Geronimo?

described his birthplace as located near the headwaters of the Gila River. Although scholars now believe that Geronimo spoke using the old nomenclature (which would put his birthplace near the present Clifton, Arizona, and the confluence of the Blue and Gila Rivers), it was once held that the chief was born near the hot spring not far from the modern Gila headwaters in New Mexico.

If it's a stretch of the imagination to believe that Geronimo was born at the mineral spring a half-mile north of the confluence of the West and Middle Forks of the Gila, the feared warrior certainly passed by the spring many times, perhaps stopping briefly to ease into the soothing water before hustling on. Several Apache trails converged near the Gila Forks, as the river bottoms offered the tribe the only passage through the rugged Mogollon Mountains. Hot springs along the Middle Fork of the Gila River probably soothed the aches of many of the great Apache chiefs such as Victorio, Mangas Coloradas, and Cochise. As evidence of their use, in 1885, the remains of a *wicki-up*—a low, conical Apache hut—were found over the spring. Made of bent willow sticks with one end stuck fast in the ground, the dome-shaped shelter was used for sweat baths, which were an important cleansing rite for the Apaches.

The mark of the Apaches runs deep throughout the Gila region, including in the name itself. Since its first appearance in a Spanish journal of 1634, *Gila* has been identified as a Spanish corruption of an Apache word. Most likely it was derived from *tsihl,* the Apache word for mountain. Indeed, the land of the Apaches is rugged, mountainous terrain.

For modern adventurers, Lightfeather Hot Spring serves as an ideal introduction to the primitive springs of the Gila Wilderness. The short walk to the spring provides a glimpse at what is required to reach more remote springs. In the Gila region, hiking means repeatedly fording rivers. Any canyon trip in the Gila will force you into the water from five to ten times per mile. Proper footwear is critical to prevent sore feet. Wading on the gravel-and-cobble river bottoms in bare feet is unpleasant, especially when you must make fifty crossings in the course of a day. Stopping to remove your boots, wade, then replace your footwear at every

Thermal and river water mix to create pleasant soaking temperatures at Lightfeather Hot Spring.

crossing will definitely slow you down. The simplest alternative is to hike in high-top running shoes with a pair of tight-fitting socks. Some hikers prefer to wade in their hiking boots, and the low humidity and high heat of the desert air serve to dry out boots quickly, but this technique can lead to blistered feet. My preference is to hike in all-terrain sandals and a pair of padded hiking socks. The sandals offer secure footing, a solid sole, and are completely amphibious. If you plan to hike to some of the remote Gila springs, experiment with several options to find which alternative best suits your own hiking style.

Lightfeather Hot Spring is only a short walk from the Gila Visitor Center, but the half-mile trip forces you to ford the river twice. You won't be able to reach the spring in times of high water. Generally, high flows occur only during runoff, which, depending on snowpack and spring temperatures, occurs from mid-March to early to mid-May. The Middle Fork can also run high following severe summer thunderstorms.

From the backcountry parking area located to the left and behind the Gila Visitor Center, look for the signs pointing to the Middle Fork Trail 157 and the Gila Wilderness. Once on the trail, walk downhill to the Middle Fork. Almost immediately, the trail crosses the river, where depending on the flow, the water can be from calf- to thigh-deep. Continue on the west bank for the next quarter-mile, then make another river crossing. The spring is found directly on the trail along the east bank.

Hot water issues from the ground along a cliff below a low-ceilinged cave shelter. The 130-degree water flows in a steaming stream before pooling in several mud-bottomed tubs that are too hot to enjoy. Two or three rock-lined pools from 4 to 10 feet in diameter are found in the bed of the river, and here thermal and river water mix to create pleasant soaking temperatures in shallow tubs. You might find it necessary to realign a few cobbles to let in more cool water from the river before sitting in the gravel-bottomed pools.

With at least five tubs, Lightfeather Hot Spring can accommodate more than a dozen soakers, but curiously, despite their easy access, I've never seen the pools crowded. However, Lightfeather Hot Spring is located right on the Middle Fork Trail, and backpackers frequently tramp by on their way up the canyon. You'll rarely enjoy this spring in solitude, and you'll certainly want to follow Forest Service regulations on bathing attire. Campsites are limited in the area of the spring, so this trip is more suitable for day hiking than for an overnight stay.

The Gila Forks are located a considerable distance from the nearest town, Silver City. You'll find campgrounds at Gila Hot Springs and small Forest Service areas along the road to Gila Cliff Dwellings National Monument. It's a good idea to lay in a supply of food and gas in Silver City before heading to the Forks country. You can pick up the basics at the trading post in Gila Hot Springs.

Give Lightfeather Hot Spring a try before venturing to the more remote springs in the Gila Wilderness. You'll find yourself eager for more desert canyon experiences.

19. Jordan Hot Spring

(*Also known as Jordan Canyon Hot Spring, House Log Canyon Hot Spring*)
Location: northwest of the Gila Visitor Center in the Gila Wilderness
Type: a primitive hot spring along the Middle Fork of the Gila River
Services: none. Basic services are found at Gila Hot Springs, 4 miles to the east; other services are 42 miles away in Silver City.
Temperature: 94°F   **Discharge:** 1 gpm   **Elevation:** 5,980 feet
Hike Rating: moderate, 12 to 16 miles round-trip
Maps: USGS Woodland Park 7.5' quadrangle (not shown on map)

Trailhead Access: From the intersection of US Highway 180 and New Mexico Highway 15 (Pinos Altos Road) in Silver City, take New Mexico Highway 15 north toward Gila Cliff Dwellings National Monument. Travel is slow on this narrow, winding road and it will take at least an hour and a half to drive 42 miles to the Gila Visitor Center. For the Middle Fork Trail access, park in the backcountry parking area located to the left and behind the Visitor Center. For the Little Bear Canyon Trail, turn left just before reaching the Visitor Center and head toward Gila Cliff Dwellings. Drive 1 mile to the TJ Corral Trailhead, which is just past the bridge over the West Fork.

A t the northern end of the line of thermal springs found deep in the Gila Wilderness lies the Meadows Warm Spring. Low flows and lukewarm temperatures keep most would-be soakers away. Instead, backcountry hot-spring enthusiasts head for the sublime, shaded pool of Jordan Hot Spring.

You have a choice of routes to reach Jordan Hot Spring, but the minimum round-trip hike is 12 miles. The shortest route leads over a dry mesa and down Little Bear Canyon to the Middle Fork, then up that river to the springs—a 6-mile, one-way hike. The longer, more scenic route follows the Middle Fork from the Visitor Center to Little Bear Canyon and beyond to the springs, an 8-mile trip.

The short route to Jordan Hot Spring begins at the TJ Corral Trailhead. Begin walking on Trail 729, following the signs for Little

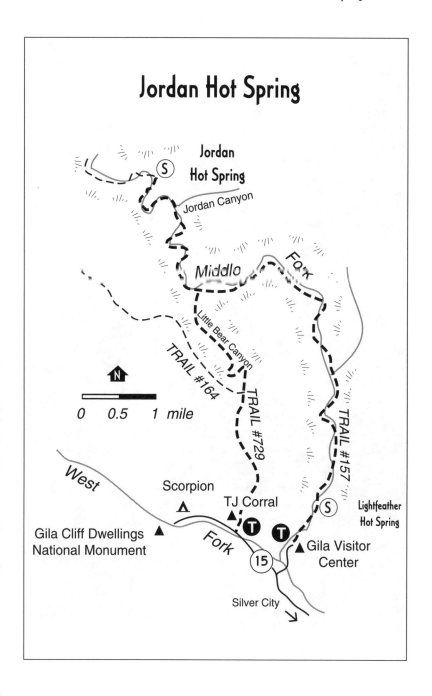

Jordan Hot Spring

Jordan Hot Spring (S)

Jordan Canyon

Middle Fork

Little Bear Canyon

TRAIL #164

TRAIL #729

TRAIL #157

N

0   0.5   1 mile

West

Scorpion

TJ Corral

Lightfeather Hot Spring (S)

Gila Cliff Dwellings National Monument

Fork

15

Gila Visitor Center

Silver City

Little Bear Canyon is the shortest route to Jordan Hot Spring.

Bear Canyon and the Middle Fork. The trail ascends a sloping mesa, parallel to Adobe Canyon to the west. The open woodlands can make for a hot hike, so start early in the day, carry plenty of water, and take advantage of the meager shade provided by the juniper and piñon pines along the trail. Over the first 2 miles the trail gradually gains 800 feet. Just past the junction with Trail 164 heading to the Meadows, reach a small pass and begin a serpentine descent into Little Bear Canyon. You'll soon be under tall pines as you walk down the narrowing canyon. The last half-mile before the Middle Fork is through a lush, confined slice in the rocks where yellow columbines and monkey flowers light up the canyon walls. The canyon here is so narrow that it poses a danger during flash floods, so keep an eye on the weather. Four miles from the start, reach the junction with the Middle Fork Trail. The river is just beyond, and you'll find several shady campsites nearby.

You can also reach the junction of Little Bear Canyon and the Middle Fork via the wet route by taking the Middle Fork Trail 157 from the Visitor Center. From the backcountry parking area, follow a wide road down to the river and make the first of about thirty crossings necessary to reach Little Bear Canyon. Late spring through fall, each crossing will be from calf- to thigh-deep, but the currents are gentle and the crossings not difficult. You'll pass Lightfeather Hot Spring in a half-mile and soon enter a world of soaring walls of orange rhyolite. Between crossings, the trail crosses sandy flats, often under the shade of spreading sycamores. The junction with Little Bear Canyon is 6 miles from the trailhead.

From Little Bear Canyon, continue upstream on the Middle Fork Trail. You'll want to count stream crossings—it's the best way to locate Jordan Hot Spring. The first of fifteen river crossings is only a splash away from the trail junction. For the next 2.5 miles between the junction and the spring, the trail and river wind together through a half-dozen broad bends. Along the way, Big Bear Canyon enters from the right and the dry Jordan Canyon from the left. Two miles from the junction, the river turns south, then swings to the north in a sweeping meander. Soon after

Backpackers cross the Middle Fork of the Gila River below Jordan Hot Spring.

making the fifteenth crossing, pass a marshy area to the right and step over a couple of warm rivulets flowing from the slope above. Just before what would be the sixteenth crossing, the trail crosses a small warm pool just below the main spring.

The log-and-rock pool at Jordan Hot Spring is about the most perfect soaking tub you could ask for. Around 20 feet in diameter, the pool holds 94-degree water issuing from the rocks just above. The sand-and-gravel bottom seems as comfortable as a plush sofa. The water is up to 3 feet deep. A relaxing soak in the friendly confines of this pool is a just reward after the long hike in.

Despite the distance from the trailhead, Jordan Hot Spring is a popular spot, and it is a rare time when you'll have the luxury of enjoying the pool alone. Because there is only one spring with a developed pool, be courteous of other users and be prepared to limit your soak so that others may partake of the soothing waters.

Campsites are located on many of the benches and sand bars in the canyon of the Middle Fork. Over the years, the area near Jordan Hot Spring has been hit hard by a multitude of users and the Forest Service wisely requests that backpackers not camp in the immediate vicinity of the spring but move at least 400 yards away. By moving your camp at least a quarter-mile upstream or downstream from the spring, you can help reduce erosion near the spring, stop degradation of water quality because of the high concentration of human waste, and maintain the privacy of bathers.

Chances are that once you enter the canyon of the Middle Fork, you will find it so enticing that you won't want to hurry back to civilization. If you have the time, I recommend that you combine the two trails to Jordan Hot Spring into a delightful loop hike. Take the Little Bear Canyon route from TJ Corral to the spring, then follow the Middle Fork back to the trailhead for a 14-mile trip. You can either walk the road or a half-mile long but difficult-to-find cutoff from the Visitor Center back to TJ Corral.

Jordan Hot Spring is the Gila Wilderness' best family hot-spring destination. The 12-mile round-trip means most families will have to backpack into the wilderness for at least one night, preferably two. The easiest way to make the trip is to use the Little Bear Canyon Trail and camp near where the trail meets the Middle Fork, then hike to the spring the following day. After another night in the canyon, return via the Middle Fork Trail. The multitude of stream crossings serves to keep kids constantly amused. Bullfrog tadpoles as thick as a thumb, cattails, hawks, and an abundance of wildflowers make the hike along the Middle Fork a delight for kids of all ages.

While you are in the area, don't miss the opportunity to visit Gila Cliff Dwellings National Monument, 1.5 miles from the Gila Visitor Center. A 1-mile trail leads up an intimate side canyon of the West Fork and into a tremendous sheltering overhang that protects several large multistoried housing complexes from the Mogollon culture that are more than six hundred years old.

20. Turkey Creek Hot Springs

Location: about 30 miles northwest of Silver City
Type: primitive springs in a remote desert canyon
Services: none. Nearest basic services are at the towns of Gila and Cliff, 14 miles away on rough roads; other services are 39 miles southeast in Silver City
Temperature: 165°F **Discharge:** 2 to 10 gpm **Elevation:** 5,100 feet
Hike Rating: difficult, 8 miles round-trip
Maps: USGS Canyon Hill 7.5' quadrangle (springs not shown on map)

Trailhead Access: From Silver City, take US 180 west for 25 miles to New Mexico Highway 211 and turn right toward the town of Gila. In 4 miles, continue straight onto New Mexico Highway 153 when New Mexico Highway 211 bears left. The pavement ends in another 4 miles as the road becomes Forest Road 155.

Forest Road 155 is rough and has several steep sections, but under good conditions, it can be traveled by carefully driven passenger cars. Before starting out, give the Silver City Ranger District a call ([505] 538-2771) and inquire about road conditions. Travel is slow as the road

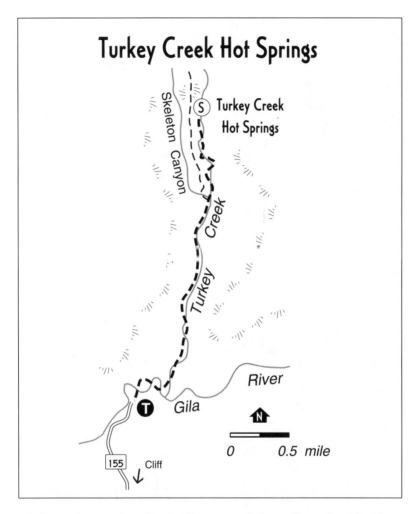

Turkey Creek Hot Springs

Skeleton Canyon

(S) Turkey Creek
Hot Springs

Turkey Creek

River

T Gila

N

0   0.5 mile

155 Cliff

winds over a pass into Brushy Canyon and descends to the Gila River. Follow the main road to the end, which is 9.5 miles from the end of the pavement, and park in one of the pullouts near the river. The trip from US Highway 180 to the river takes about one hour.

Hidden in a picturesque desert canyon, Turkey Creek Hot Springs is New Mexico's premier backcountry hot-water destination. Turkey Creek flows beneath a cool canopy of walnut and

Hidden in a picturesque desert canyon, Turkey Creek Hot Springs is New Mexico's premier backcountry hot water destination.

sycamore trees wedged between ragged walls of orange rock. As the rippling water melts around boulders and over slickrock terraces, the canyon seems like a bit of paradise that slipped from the hands of the Creator and plopped down in the middle of the sun-blasted, hellish desert slopes of the Mogollon Mountains.

The earliest record of Turkey Creek Hot Springs comes from a story told to Gila pioneer Jack Stockbridge by old-timer Noah Owens. Owens was stationed at nearby Fort West in the early 1860s when two men rode into the fort from the nearby mountains. The men said their party had been attacked by Apaches, and they were the only survivors. They escaped through the canyons of the Gila River before being forced from the river by cliffs and quicksand. Riding over the first ridge, they dropped into Turkey Creek Canyon, finding and camping by the hot springs. The next morning, they found signs of gold, headed down Turkey Creek to the Gila, and then on to the fort.

After wintering in Arizona, the two returned to mine the gold. At Fort West, they were emphatically warned against going back into the mountains because of the presence of a large number of Apaches. With eyes lit up by gold fever, the two ignored the soldiers' warnings. The fort commander agreed to send the men off with a small escort. The soldiers stayed with the gold-seekers for several miles up Turkey Creek before heading downstream to return to the fort. Within minutes of leaving the prospectors, the escort heard shots ring out from up the canyon. They rode back to find the two men had been killed by Apaches at the mouth of Skeleton Canyon.

It's no easy trip to reach the hot springs. From the end of the road, 3 miles of trail and 1 mile of boulder-hopping remain. You must wade across the Gila River several times, and do a bit of route-finding to reach Turkey Creek. Although the 8-mile round-trip is possible to do in a day, you'll want to savor the experience of the canyon and the springs by spending a night in the Gila Wilderness. If you choose to backpack in, be prepared to carry your pack over a rough, trail-less mile. Pack light.

High flows of the Gila River can block access to the mouth of

Turkey Creek during runoff. In summer there is the threat of flash floods in the narrow canyon. At this low elevation, summer temperatures can peak at more than 100 degrees. Early to mid-May and fall are the best times to make the trip.

The first mile of the hike from the trailhead is a bit confusing. From the berm at the end of the road, walk along the river to a washout, then follow a short trail to pick up the road once again. Continue to the first ford of the Gila River. (You'll notice tire tracks in the sand and locals do drive across the river, but it is not recommended.) Wade the knee-deep water and continue on the road across a wide gravel bar on the north bank. In another quarter mile, ford the river again and walk the sandy road to a third crossing of the Gila. Across the river, continue on the track straight ahead, ignoring the main road angling off to the right.

The point of land between Turkey Creek and the Gila River holds a spider web of connected dirt tracks. Try to stay on the well-worn track that parallels the base of the cliff on the left. Walk across the point of land to the rocky, dry bed of Turkey Creek. Angle left up the stream bed for 100 feet, then follow an old road past several old buildings. Just past a windmill, a trail sign points the way across the now-flowing Turkey Creek. If you miss the trail or get confused, walk east across the point of land to the dry bed of Turkey Creek. Follow the creek bed upstream and watch the banks until you pick up the obvious trail that crosses the stream about 0.3 miles above the Gila.

Once on the obvious trail, walk up canyon under oaks and alligator junipers. For the next mile, Turkey Creek flows intermittently first to the right, then the left. After crossing the Gila Wilderness boundary, the canyon narrows and the walk is a bit cooler. Almost 2 miles above the river, the trail splits, with one branch climbing very steeply over a low cliff, and the other staying along the creek before they rejoin in 100 yards. Just after the split, the canyon widens and the trail enters a shady forest. In a few minutes, the trail turns west to head up Skeleton Canyon. As the trail starts uphill, watch for rock cairns that mark the route that continues up Turkey

Soaking it up in the largest pool at Turkey Creek.

Creek. If you start climbing steep switchbacks or continue west up Skeleton Canyon, backtrack to stay near Turkey Creek.

With the maintained trail behind you, the route up Turkey Creek is a rugged one. Well-worn social trails are found for part of the way, but mostly you'll be boulder-hopping up canyon. The most-used path crosses the stream on stepping stones, dives through rock tunnels, and hangs on ledges. Several parallel routes can be found at various levels on the east bank. In general, pick your way as best you can. The following directions may be of some help.

After a few minutes of walking above the junction with Skeleton Canyon, you'll pass under an overhang near a slickrock ledge. Around the next bend, a deep pool forces the trail to go under a rockfall—you'll have to drag your pack through the tunnel. After passing some deep swimming holes, you'll need to watch for an alcove in the east canyon wall where a dry side canyon enters Turkey Creek. At this point, you are about a quarter-mile from the hot springs.

After the alcove, watch for trails on the east bank of the stream. You might reach one point where it seems impossible to continue up canyon near the stream; from that point, backtrack about 100 feet and look for a faint trail leading up and over the rock obstacle. When you notice thick algae growth in the stream, you'll know the water temperature is distinctly warmer than down below. A campsite alcove on the west bank marks the lowest of the hot seeps coming from the rocks.

Many would-be bathers have called this spring difficult to locate. I suggest carrying the USGS Canyon Hill quadrangle map. On the map, the springs are located along the creek between the 5,780-foot point on the ridge between Sycamore and Turkey Creeks and the 5,200 label on the contour line to the east.

Hot springs are found along about 200 yards of canyon bottom. None of the springs have much flow, but thermal water seeps from under the sand along the stream, from cracks in the rocks, and from short side canyons. You may find a few rock-lined pools where spring and stream water mix, but these are usually washed out by the tremendous spring floods that roar down the canyon. Soaking pools range from hot to cool and from hot-tub-sized to one incredible swimming hole more than 8 feet deep.

Just above the springs, the canyon broadens, affording a few small campsites on low benches above the river. If you've got your backpack this far, you're in for a delightful stay. Combined with soaring canyon walls and slickrock terraces, the hot springs are just one part of the experience of Turkey Creek. The patterns of rock and water flowing beneath the shady canopy of trees invite exploring upstream. Trout swim in the cooler water above the springs. It's one of New Mexico's most enchanting places.

Despite the effort required to reach the springs, they receive a fair number of visitors each year, so don't expect to have the canyon and the thermal water to yourself. You'll especially want to treat Turkey Creek with the respect that it's due so that this unique spot can be fully enjoyed by others.

21. San Francisco Hot Spring and Lower Frisco Hot Spring

(*Also known as Lower Frisco Hot Spring, Upper Frisco Hot Springs*)

Location: 56 miles northwest of Silver City, 5 miles south of Glenwood in the Gila National Forest

Type: a primitive spring on the banks of the San Francisco River

Services: none. Nearest basic services are in Glenwood, 5 miles away; other services are located 58 miles southeast in Silver City.

Temperature: 98 to 114°F

Discharge: 1 to 37 gpm

Elevation: 4,550 feet

Hike Rating: easy, 2 miles round trip

Maps: USGS Wilson Mountain 7.5' quadrangle

Trailhead Access: From the intersection of New Mexico Highway 90 and US Highway 180 in Silver City, take US Highway 180 west toward Glenwood. In about 56 miles, coincidentally just past milepost 56, turn left onto Forest Road 519. The turnoff is located a mile south of Pleasanton and 5 miles south of Glenwood. Forest Road 519 is a well-maintained gravel road suitable for all vehicles. In just over a half-mile, take the right fork (the left fork leads to private land). If the road ahead seems too rough for your vehicle, park and continue on foot. Follow the road to the end of the wide cobble camping and parking area along the river.

The convoluted course of the San Francisco River begins near Alpine, Arizona, and ends at the Gila River near Clifton in the same state. Between the two ends, the river snakes into New Mexico for more than 100 miles. A dozen miles before it returns to Arizona, a series of hot springs stretch along a half-mile of the San Francisco River.

The main spring takes its name from the river and has long been identified as San Francisco Hot Spring. A major spring located several hundred yards downstream is often, but confusingly, called the Upper Spring. Its location downstream from San

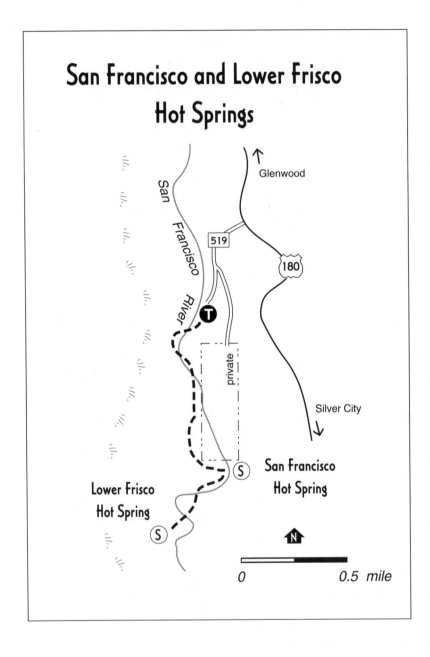

San Francisco and Lower Frisco Hot Springs

Francisco Hot Spring makes it more properly called the Lower Spring.

San Francisco Hot Spring achieved its first fame as a stop on the Silver City to Alma stagecoach route. A small bathhouse was constructed at the site by an unknown entrepreneur, but with the small flow volumes and no nearby railroad, development at the site was kept to a minimum.

Recent changes have shut down the road leading directly to San Francisco Hot Spring, and now you must hike to reach it. It is no more than a quarter-mile from the parking area to the spring, but cliffs force you into the water twice along the way. During high water in spring or following heavy summer thunderstorms, enjoyment of this set of springs is limited to the upper group. Do not attempt to reach the springs when the river is running high. Even if you attempted the trip, you'd be disappointed: At high flows, the springs are covered by the river.

From the south end of the parking area, locate a trail that crosses the river near the black cliffs. You'll ford to an island, walk south a few minutes, then cross the other half of the river to the true west bank. Almost immediately, cross the full river back to the east bank near a stream gauge. The trail follows an old road, but you need to avoid a section of private land by walking close to or in the river—a refreshing trip from late spring to fall. Watch for signs and old truck tires marking the boundary and stay on public land.

Just beyond where the old access road comes down from the bluffs, a cluster of tall cottonwoods marks a once-maintained Forest Service picnic area, which now is often adopted as home by several campers. Below the picnic area lies the hottest and largest spring in the area, San Francisco Hot Spring.

Users have created a well-engineered series of pools that put the thermal water flowing from the spring to the best possible use. Four or five pools of varying temperatures lead off from the main vent, but a collection of smaller vents adds hot water to each pool. Two very hot pools that support colonies of orange and deep green

San Francisco Hot Spring is one of a series of hot springs that stretches along a half-mile section of the San Francisco River.

algae start the sequence. Next is a 15-foot-by-6-foot pool where hot water is mixed with river water to create a pleasantly warm bath. Downstream and near the bank, you'll find a long swimming hole of lukewarm water up to 4 feet deep. When humans are absent, the hole is a favorite hangout of incredibly fat carp and Sonoran suckers. Combined, the pools can hold up to twenty bathers. Many bathers choose to go without suits, but the Forest Service often issues citations for this violation of regulations.

Hot springs line up along the east bank of the river for the next half-mile downstream. The springs are small and are usually ignored by bathers. The presence of additional springs in the river bed itself can be inferred from the water temperature of the river. Above San Francisco Hot Spring, the chilly flow stays cool enough to support trout; below the spring, enough thermal water enters the river to increase the temperature up to 10 degrees, which is enough to make life difficult for trout.

The series of springs along the river reaches a climax with Lower Frisco Hot Spring, or as it is commonly called, The Bubbles. From San Francisco Hot Spring, cross the river, and you'll soon pick up an old road on the west bank leading down canyon. Follow the road across the river twice more, winding up on the west bank.

Once just any other hot spring pooling along the west bank, Lower Frisco has been transformed, and in the process, has become a New Age vortex—purportedly the site of channelized energy released from the earth. However, rather than being a random act of the cosmos, the new, much deeper, wonderfully fun pool is a product of one of the periodic floods that race down the San Francisco River, frequently altering the river's course. A few years back, high flows scoured a huge pothole at the base of a breccia cliff, deposited a broad sandbar, and rerouted the river to the eastern half of the canyon. The result was the formation of a basin at the spring that filled with warm water.

If there have been no recent floods, you should have no trouble finding The Bubbles. Looking like a platoon of short, dieting

It's claimed by some that this "vortex" near Lower Frisco Hot Spring is the site of the channelized energy being released by the earth.

aliens, dozens of 2-foot-high towers made from rounded river cobbles, and constructed with an admirable sense of balance, surround the vortex that holds the spring.

The 30-foot, roughly oval pool at the base of the cliff is up to 5 feet deep, large enough for several families. A canopy of cottonwoods provides shade overhead, and tiny bubbles from the underwater vents will tickle your feet as you soak. Several rock benches provide seats above the gravel and mud bottom. It might not be a place of cosmic significance, but the pool offers a great bath and is a fine swimming hole to boot.

The San Francisco River Canyon surrounding the springs is as delightful a canyon as any in the Gila. The walls are spread apart enough to present wide vistas of the volcanic cliffs that border the river. The clear water slips over riffles and turns glassy in the pools, reflecting the breezy riparian vegetation and the contrasting cliffs. The broad canyon floor provides an abundance of primitive campsites. Avoid the many sites near the springs that show signs of abuse. Select previously used sites, preferably downstream from the springs, that have been properly cared for.

As New Age believers have adopted the springs and spread word of its location, the thermal features and the surrounding area have received a wide variety of users and abusers. Some thermal water worshippers are essentially homesteading nearby. It adds up to be a grand headache for the Forest Service. As a result, rumors circulate constantly that the springs will be shut down to public use. Before you visit the San Francisco River hot spring area, give the Glenwood Ranger Station a call ([505] 539-2481), and check out the current status of the area.

If the springs are open, you're in for a delightful trip into a sensitive desert canyon. Enjoy both the river and the thermal features, sharing them courteously with others, and leaving the canyon in the same condition as you found it.

22. Frisco Box Hot Spring

(*Also known as Upper Frisco Hot Spring, Frisco Hot Spring*)
Location: 10 miles northeast of Luna in the Gila National Forest
Type: a primitive spring on the banks of the San Francisco River
Services: none. Nearest basic services are in Luna 18 miles away; other
   services in Reserve, New Mexico, and Alpine, Arizona, each
   about 25 miles.
Temperature: 98°F   **Discharge:** 7 gpm   **Elevation:** 6,530 feet
Hike Rating: strenuous, 6 miles round-trip
Maps: USGS Dillon Mountain 7.5' quadrangle, identified as Frisco Hot
   Spring

Trailhead Access: From Luna, head south and east on US 180 about 6
miles to Forest Road 35 and turn left. From the south, Forest Road 35 is
located about 7 miles north of the intersection of US 180 and New Mexico Highway 12. Take the winding, all-weather gravel Forest Road 35 for
12 miles, of which the last 4 miles can be rough and require a high-clearance vehicle. Drive to the end of the road at H Bar V Saddle and park at
the trailhead sign. Check road conditions at the Quemado Ranger District before heading out.

The Frisco Box and its hot spring are among the most delightful
places in all of New Mexico. The spring is located in the peaceful valley of the San Francisco River about a mile before the river
plunges through a tumultuous gorge. The contrast is exquisite
and has always made this area one of the premier hiking destinations in the entire state.

Alas, here is another tale of woe for hikers, anglers, and hot-
spring enthusiasts. The road to the easiest, most-used trailhead
for the hot spring and the canyon has been closed by a private
landowner. In the past, the owner has permitted access along Cen-
terfire Creek to the trailhead located just inside the Gila National
Forest boundary. The road on this private in-holding was closed
in 1996 and remains so as I write. The closure, which will likely be

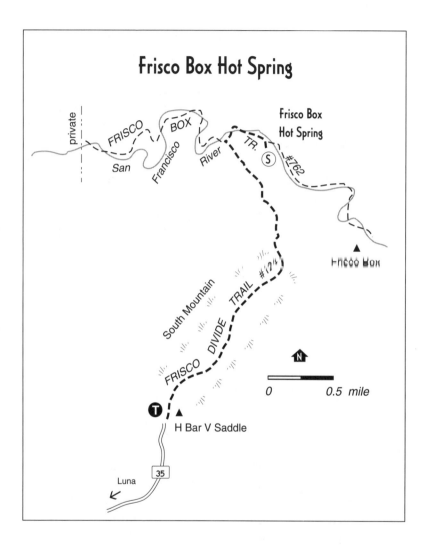

Frisco Box Hot Spring

permanent, is the result of years of disrespectful treatment of the private land that culminated in a verbal conflict between the landowner and an outdoor recreationist. UNDER NO CIRCUM-STANCES SHOULD YOU USE THIS ACCESS.

Fortunately, there is an alternative access, but you must be a reasonably strong and experienced hiker to use it. Access to the

Frisco Box Hot Spring is via Forest Road 35 and Frisco Divide Trail 124. The trail will take you from the road to the hot spring in 3 miles, dropping 1,600 feet on the way. The difficulty, of course, lies in the steep climb back to the parking area. It's a huffer, especially after you let the warm water of the spring relax your muscles.

The route requires two river crossings, which means access to Frisco Box Hot Spring can be blocked by high water. Spring runoff and an occasional summer thunderstorm swell the flow of the river to dangerous levels, and hikers must stay away during these times. Suitable water levels usually occur from mid-May through October. In winter, deep snow closes Forest Road 35.

Don't attempt the steep and rocky trip from H Bar V Saddle to the river in your river-crossing shoes. The rigors of the hike demand that you wear sturdy hiking boots for the trail to the river. Once on the Frisco Box Trail at the river, you can change into footwear suitable for making the required river crossings. Also, be warned that the trail receives light use, is not regularly maintained, and is frequently difficult to follow. If you aren't experienced in the backcountry, don't attempt this hike.

From the trailhead on H Bar V Saddle, begin walking north on the Frisco Divide Trail. Make a brief climb to the ridge line of South Mountain and enjoy the views of the San Francisco River far below. The trail stays on the ridge top for the first 1.5 miles, following the swales of the rocks. At the point of the ridge, it drops down into the conifer forest. The trail switchbacks steeply down the north slope of the mountain, offering a cool walk in summer. Watch carefully for the trail. Continue dropping for another mile, then reach Frisco Box Trail 762. Turn right onto the Frisco Box Trail and walk parallel to the river, downstream. Make two easy river crossings, then start watching for a side trail that leads to the hot spring, which is located about a quarter-mile from the junction of the two main trails.

The spring is on the south bank of the river and a sign usually points the way from the trail to the spring. Walk to the right across the sandbar two or three minutes to reach the thermal outlet.

If you look around, you can find at least four seeps where hot water reaches the surface. The warm water from the largest vent is collected in a concrete box that sits on a bench about 30 feet above river level. The box is 4 feet by 8 feet and about 18 inches deep. The rough bottom is not the most comfortable surface, but the thermal water holds at a perfect, warm temperature and the view of the surrounding mountains is spectacular.

You shouldn't make the trip to Frisco Box Hot Spring without taking a peek at the entrance to the spring's namesake about a mile below. After miles of flowing through a broad valley, the San Francisco River plunges suddenly into a wild canyon barely wide enough for itself. Granite cliffs jump up from the water and boulders choke the narrow bottom of the gorge. Traveling very far beyond the entrance means getting wet and may well require swimming. Even if you make it only as far as the entrance, the view downstream is unforgettable.

There is a bright side to the closure of the river-level access road: The added difficulty of reaching the hot spring has drastically reduced visitation and created a true backcountry mineral bath with few rivals in New Mexico. The soak in the pool, with its attendant views, is ample reward for the hike in. Plan on spending a day along the San Francisco River, or make the trip into a short backpack. You're likely to find that you have a little piece of paradise all to yourself.

23. Gila Hot Springs Vacation Center

Location: 39 miles north of Silver City near the confluence of the East and West Forks of the Gila River

Type: developed hot pools in a primitive setting on the banks of the West Fork of the Gila River

Services: camping, lodging, country store, showers, and natural hot pools near the Gila River

Temperature: 150°F, cooled to about 108°F
Discharge: up to 200 gpm   **Elevation:** 5,600 feet
Address: Gila Hot Springs, Rt. 11, Silver City, NM 88061
Phone: (505) 536-9551
Maps: USGS Gila Hot Springs 7.5' quadrangle

How to Get There: From the intersection of US Highway 180 and New Mexico Highway 15 (Pinos Altos Road) in Silver City, take New Mexico Highway 15 north toward Gila Cliff Dwellings National Monument. Travel is slow on this narrow, winding road and it will take at least an hour and a half to drive 37.5 miles to the Upper Gila River Bridge. Cross the bridge and continue 1.2 miles to Access Road. Turn right onto this gravel road, driving slowly downhill toward the river. In 0.2 miles, turn left onto West Fork Road. In a few hundred yards, bear right to enter the campground. After registering, find the hot pools to the right near the discharge pipe.

L ocated at the gateway to the Gila Wilderness, the Gila Hot Springs Vacation Center is an outpost of civilization set deep in the mountains. Surrounded by desert hills, the center, set on the banks of the cool-flowing West Fork of the Gila River, is a breath of fresh air. You can have wilderness-like experience in the comfort of your RV or a spacious apartment, all the while enjoying water from one of the great mineral springs in the Southwest.

Like the other hot springs along the forks of the Gila, the Apaches used Gila Hot Springs for centuries before the arrival of the Spanish and Americans, and the remains of a single low wall at the springs may date from this period. Trapper James Ohio Pattie probably soaked in these springs in December, 1824, before heading up the West Fork, looking for beaver. But Apache territory wasn't a safe place during the middle decades of the nineteenth century, and it was only during lulls in the continuing wars that travelers could relax in the springs. During this period, soldiers from an outpost near the confluence of the East and West Forks built a rough shelter over one of the springs.

As gold and silver were discovered and mined from the hills in the Silver City area in the 1860s, miners from Pinos Altos,

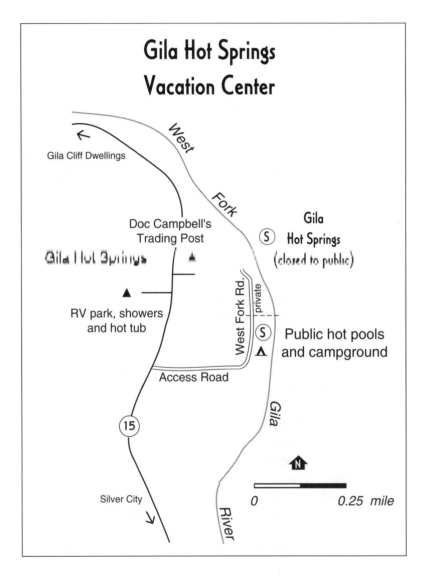

Gila Hot Springs Vacation Center

Gila Cliff Dwellings

West Fork

Doc Campbell's Trading Post

Gila Hot Springs

Gila Hot Springs (closed to public)

West Fork Rd.

private

RV park, showers and hot tub

Public hot pools and campground

Access Road

15

Gila

Silver City

River

N

0   0.25 mile

Kingston, and other mining towns came to Gila Hot Springs to enjoy the water. Around 1870, John Perry lived at the springs, offering baths to miners and farming the fertile ground surrounding the Gila forks.

By the time of the Silver City mining boom in the 1880s, Geronimo and his band were off to Mexico and the mountains were safe for travelers. Gila Hot Springs was then owned by the Hill brothers, who were smart enough to cater their mineral baths to miners who came to soak out their aches and pains. To encourage visitors, the brothers maintained a 16-mile road from Sapillo Creek to the springs. The Hills dug out deep pools on the slope above the West Fork, built an adobe bathhouse over each pool, and piped in hot water. To add to the allure of their mountain retreat, they advertised the boundless hunting and fishing opportunities in the rich country of the Gila forks.

When most of the mines played out, visitation to the springs dropped to near nothing. Through the first decades of the twentieth century, only a handful of local ranchers used the springs.

Doc Campbell is something of a legend in the Gila Wilderness. Coming from Pennsylvania around 1935, Campbell ranched and guided hunting trips in the canyons, exploring perhaps more of the wilderness than anyone else. In 1940, he and his wife, Ida, purchased a sizable property that included the travertine deposits of Gila Hot Springs, thus beginning his more than fifty-five-year association with the land. Campbell tapped the hot springs to supply hot water to the ranch and advertised the springs as a natural spa. While ranching the surrounding country, Campbell ran an outfitting business and was made the first custodian of Gila Cliff Dwellings National Monument. Campbell still lives at Gila Hot Springs in the simple adobe ranch house he built in the 1940s. Three of his children remain on the ranch and run the businesses.

Begin your visit to Gila Hot Springs Vacation Center at Doc Campbell's Trading Post located 1.4 miles north of the Upper Gila River Bridge. The trading post has supplies ranging from groceries to ice to books on local history. The friendly staff, mostly part of the Campbell family, will answer your questions and steer you in the right direction to the springs or any of the other attractions in the surrounding country.

You have several options for staying at the Vacation Center. An

Doc Campbell's Trading Post offers a friendly welcome to the Gila Hot Springs Vacation Center.

RV park is located near the store and boasts hot and cold water taps at all hookups. The hot water is piped in from the hot springs, so you can enjoy mineral water in your own camper. The daily, weekly, and monthly rates are very reasonable. You can also rent a comfortable apartment with kitchenette or a spacious trailer. If you have a tent, the riverside campground is right on the West Fork and by the hot springs, and the fee is nominal. All the lodgings are provided with mineral water from the springs. Reservations are recommended for accommodations.

Gila Hot Springs proper cover a huge expanse of hillside with gray, weathered travertine cascading down the slope in a series of terraces. The springs are located on top of a fault, and the thermal water issues from fractures in the rhyolite cliff from river level to 30 feet above. The water is hot—up to 150 degrees—and has a relatively low amount of dissolved minerals. The springs are too hot for bathing and are located on private land not open to the public.

Water is piped from the hot springs to three riverside pools located at the campground. To soak in the spring-fed pools, drive to the campground and stop at the information board. Register there for camping or a bath or both. Fill out a form and pay the small day-use or camping fee. Find a spot under one of the towering cottonwoods, and the hot pools are just a few yards away. Observe the warning signs that the campground is surrounded by private property and stay within the limits of public-use land.

The three pools are located a few hundred yards downstream from the travertine deposits of Gila Hot Springs. Water from the springs is piped across the river, under the access road, and through an outlet in the middle of the campground. The water doesn't lose much of its heat before splashing into the first pool where orange and luminous-green algae is your first clue that the water may be uncomfortably hot. The water cools a few degrees as it reaches the second pool, but it's not until the largest, third pool that the temperature is reduced to a pleasant level.

The 20-foot-by-8-foot pool is large enough for an entire family to enjoy. The gravel-and-mud bottom makes a great seat to relax and stare up at the tan bluffs of Gila conglomerate that rise abruptly only a few yards away. From the pool, you can hear the murmur of the West Fork. Look for ravens soaring off the cliffs and warblers, goldfinches, and orioles fluttering amid the willow leaves. The pools are as close to a wilderness experience as you can have without a long hike.

If you want to soak in a bit more comfort, you'll find a hot tub waiting for you in the RV park. The RV park showers are yet another alternative. The water for both comes directly from the hot springs.

The folks at the trading post can also set you up for a wilderness adventure. They will outfit you for a hunting or fishing pack trip, a trail ride, or a guided trip to one of the nearby wilderness hot springs. If you're a hiker looking for a long wilderness trip, consider the Campbell's drop camp service.

The Gila Hot Springs Vacation Center offers something for every taste. The ease of access to thermal pools is unmatched in the Gila, but it's the down-home, neighborly atmosphere that gives the place its unique charm.

Relax away your cares in a wilderness-like setting at the large pools of the Gila Hot Springs Vacation Center.

24. Faywood Hot Springs

Location: between Silver City and Deming, next to City of Rocks State
Park
Type: a private, informal resort with public and private bathing areas
Services: baths, massage therapy, full hookup RV sites, tent sites, café,
museum, and gift shop
Temperature: 130 to 150°F   **Discharge:** at least 100 gpm
Elevation: 5,020 feet
Address: HC 71 Box 1240, 165 Hwy 61, Faywood, NM 88034
Phone: (505) 536-9663
Maps: USGS Faywood Station 7.5' quadrangle

How to Get There: From Deming, head north on US Highway 180. In
23 miles, turn right onto New Mexico Highway 61. Continue 1.6 miles
to the entrance. From the Silver City area, take US Highway 180 south.
In 25 miles, turn left onto New Mexico Highway 61. The entrance is 1.6
miles from the intersection.

A s you drive across the rolling grasslands of the Rio Mimbres
Valley north of Deming, you see it from miles away. Something isn't quite right: Ahead is a lush, green hill rising in the
midst of the swaying dry grasses and dancing plumes of yucca
flowers. Shaped like a giant anthill, the oasis of dense mesquite
and scattered hackberry can only mean one thing—water, and in
this case, hot mineral-laden water.

Eons of the evaporation of water from Faywood Hot Springs
have left a hard-to-miss 30-foot travertine mound. Writings from
the eighteenth century mention the impressive mound and a
plume of steam rising from it that could be seen for dozens of
miles. It was perhaps the steam that first led members of the Mimbres culture to the springs. More than seven hundred years ago, the
Mimbreños built a small pueblo nearby. Pieces of their exquisite
pottery, along with flint tools, arrowheads and spearheads, stone

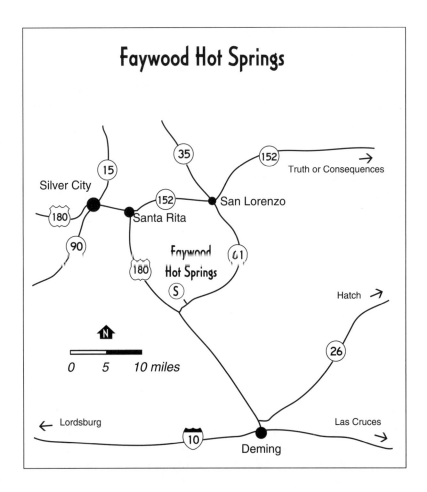

Faywood Hot Springs

Silver City

35
15
152 → Truth or Consequences
San Lorenzo
180
152
Santa Rita
90
Faywood
61
180 Hot Springs
S
Hatch ↗
N
0   5   10 miles
26
← Lordsburg
Las Cruces
10 → →
Deming

pipes, and a large variety of other artifacts, were discovered in the depths of the springs during a clean-out in 1893.

The Apaches considered the striking patch of green amid the desert, located in the heart of their territory, a favorite campsite. Only a few miles south of the long-active copper mine at Santa Rita, the Spanish, too, knew of the springs, and, as tradition would have it, they called the place Ojo Caliente.

John Bartlett passed by this verdant hot springs during his

1851 Mexican-United States border survey. As with modern visitors, he was impressed by the dimensions of the deposits surrounding the springs, which he measured at 600 feet in circumference from the base of the spring. Bartlett was pleased to find some water collecting in a pool, but was soon disappointed to find that the water was too hot for his bath.

The first development at what would become Faywood Hot Springs came in 1861 when W. Watts and A. Khune built a crude bathhouse and hotel. The springs were far from the established trails and roads of the day, and at first, visitation was limited to a few wanderers. Within a year, gold was discovered in the Pinos Altos Mountains to the northwest of the springs, and soon a stage ran twice a week between Mesilla and the gold mines, following roughly the route of today's US Highway 180. When passengers learned of the springs, they frequently requested a respite from the rigors of travel and took a brief dip in the pools. Such excursions became so frequent that the springs were made into a scheduled overnight stop. Increased business brought a succession of owners and much-needed improvements to the facilities.

Around 1872, Colonel Richard Hudson visited the springs to seek relief from gout. The enterprising Hudson was so taken by the curative powers of the springs that he bought the property to develop as a health resort. Hudson, who came to New Mexico with the California Column during the Civil War, used the money he made in mining and cattle ranching to finance the construction of a grand new hotel on the north side of the mound.

In contrast to the Victorian-style spas built at the same time in other parts of the country, Hudson respected the traditions of New Mexico and built a sprawling adobe. In keeping with the local style, the hotel was built in a square. Along the west wall were the six bathing rooms, furnished with wooden tubs and benches, and running hot water. The kitchen, dining area, and several small rooms that housed Hudson and his wife and daughter occupied the east side. The south wing held the guest rooms. Storerooms and a lounge on the north side completed the square. The restora-

The impressive Faywood Hot Springs, circa 1900. (Photo by O.C. Hinman; courtesy of the museum of New Mexico, neg. no. 14660.)

tive properties of the water and the unique charm of the building attracted visitors from around the country.

Again, transportation was the key to success. A revamped stage line connecting Texas to Los Angeles passed the resort and soon the Southern Pacific Railroad had a station nearby. Twice a day, a private stagecoach from the resort brought guests in the 5 miles from the station. By 1885, Hudson Hot Springs, as it was called in those days, was one of the most popular destinations in the Southwest.

When a savage fire destroyed the hotel in 1892, the disheartened Hudson decided to sell. The next owner, Andrew Graham, poured more than one hundred thousand dollars into building an elegant resort on the east side of the mound. His Casa de Consuelo was a sharp contrast to the homegrown flavor of Hudson's resort. Gone was the colonel's adobe style, replaced with wood and plaster that was more in keeping with the times. Instead of facing inward, a long porch encircled the new rectangular structure. Inside, the hotel had forty-eight bedrooms with something New Mexico had never seen before—private, in-room baths. These features made the hotel far out in the desert one of the most luxurious in New Mexico.

In 1900, the springs worked another miraculous cure that

Faywood Hot Springs has a unique storage system for its mineral water.

brought a new set of owners. T.C. McDermott first came to the springs to cure stomach ulcers and returned as part owner. Two of his partners, J.C. Fay and William Lockwood, combined parts of their names to give the resort a new one: Faywood Hot Springs.

For one spring season in 1899, the bathhouses took a back seat to baseball diamonds. A.G. Spaulding, one of the new investors and owner of the professional Chicago White Stockings (later to become the Cubs), brought the team to Faywood for spring training. The team shared the facilities with tourists, who from a hastily erected grandstand watched the team practice on what must have been the dustiest diamond in the history of professional baseball.

Faywood Hot Springs rode a wave of popularity into the twentieth century. As international tensions increased prior to the First World War, Camp Cody was built in nearby Deming, housing the 34th Infantry Division. Soldiers and their families were soon among the visitors to the springs.

As other investors pulled out, T.C. McDermott held on and continued to operate the hotel in grand style. Businessmen, ranchers, and miners from Deming and Silver City used the large rooms of the hotel for their social activities. McDermott continued to operate the bathhouses and sold bottled water until his death in 1946.

With McDermott gone, the buildings at Faywood fell into disrepair and were demolished in 1951. Kennecott Mining Company acquired the property in 1966 and permitted volunteers to maintain the springs as a local recreation area. Several revivals of the springs were attempted, but after the property was acquired by Phelps Dodge Corporation, the area was fenced and closed to the public.

After years of neglect, the springs are finally coming back into their own. Since 1993, new owners Wanda Fuselier and Elon Yurwit have taken up the task of rebuilding the springs so that a new generation of users can enjoy the wonderful water.

Fuselier and Yurwit are patiently returning some of the old charm to Faywood. Retaining the rustic nature that has long attracted visitors to the springs, they have refurbished the existing pools, developed a storage system for the mineral water, built privacy fences, and created a relaxed atmosphere that adds to the pleasure of the springs.

The high-quality mineral water, rich in a wide variety of trace elements, rises to the surface along the Treasure Mountain Fault, which runs northwest from near Deming to near Silver City. It issues from the volcanic rhyolite that underlies the Mimbres Valley and contains a wide range of minerals.

The position of the hot spring on top of the mound permits a unique arrangement of bathing facilities. All the baths and pools are outdoors, attractively placed among the native vegetation. Unobtrusive pine fencing separates clothing-required from clothing-optional pools. The rock-and-concrete pools are large enough for about a dozen people. Plans include the construction of a new clothing-required swimming pool warmed by spring water.

Five private tubs and one private pool are available for rental by the hour. You can regulate the water temperature in the private tubs. The private pool and one of the tubs are accessible for the physically challenged. Nearby is a dressing room, and towels and

The thermal pools at Faywood offer a chance to relax in a desert oasis.

bathing suits are rented for a minimal fee. No matter which bath you select, the water and the setting are wonderful.

The extensive grounds include RV spaces with full hookups and tent camping sites. You can also rent a comfortable travel trailer or tipi for the night. The moderate fees include use of the public facilities. You'll also find a café, museum, and gift shop at the Welcome Center. The walking trails on the grounds offer the chance for a desert stroll, and the oasis will provide the chance to see Gambel's quail, nighthawks, woodpeckers, orioles, cactus wrens, great horned owls, and other birds, as well as a wide variety of animals.

The pools are open to the public from 10 A.M. to 10 P.M.; guests staying on the grounds can use them twenty-four hours a day.

The present owners have a genuine concern for their stewardship of the springs, the water, and the historical significance of Faywood. They have enhanced this desert oasis, creating a simple, relaxing mineral bath that ranks among the best in New Mexico. Rest assured that Faywood is again in good hands.

SUGGESTED READING

Alexander, Hubert G., and Paul Reiter. *Report on the Excavation of Jemez Cave, New Mexico. School of American Research Monograph Series,* Vol. 1, no. 3. Albuquerque, N. Mex.: University of New Mexico Press, 1935.

Back, W. "Hydromythology and Ethnohydrology in the New World." *Water Resources Research* 17, no. 2 (1981):257–287.

Back, W., E.R. Landa, and L. Meeks. "Bottled Water, Spas, and Early Years of Water Chemistry." *Ground Water* 33, no. 4 (1995):605–614.

Debo, Angie. *Geronimo: The Man, His Times, His Place.* Norman, Okla.: University of Oklahoma Press, 1976.

Elliott, Michael L. *Jemez New Mexico State Monument.* Santa Fe, N. Mex.: Museum of New Mexico Press, 1993.

Evans, Max. *Long John Dunn of Taos.* Los Angeles: Westernlore Press, 1959.

Goff, F., and C.O. Grigsby. "Valles Caldera Geothermal System, New Mexico, USA." *Journal of Hydrology* 56 (1982):119–136.

Hamblin, C.A. *Science of Impurity: Water Analysis in 19th Century Britain.* Bristol, England: Adam Hilger, 1990.

Hembry, Phyllis. *The English Spa, 1560–1815: A Social History.* Rutherford, N.J.: Fairleigh Dickinson University Press, 1990.

Jones, F.A. *New Mexico Mines and Minerals.* Santa Fe, N. Mex.: New Mexico Printing Company, 1904.

Julyan, Robert. *The Place Names of New Mexico.* Albuquerque, N. Mex.: University of New Mexico Press, 1996.

Kamenetz, H.L. "History of American Spas and Hydrotherapy." In *Medical Hydrology,* edited by Sidney Licht. Baltimore, Md.: Waverly Press, 1968.

Lindgren, W. "The Hot Springs of Ojo Caliente and Their Deposits." *Economic Geology* 5, no. 1 (1910):22–27.

Loew, O. "Report on Mineralogical, Agricultural, and Chemical Conditions Observed in Portions of Colorado, New Mexico and Arizona." In *U.S. Geographical and Geological Survey West of the 100th Meridian*, by G. M. Wheeler, vol. 3, 613–627. Washington, D.C.: U.S. Government Printing Office, 1875.

Luhan, Mabel Dodge. *On the Edge of the Taos Desert.* 1937. Reprint, Albuquerque, N. Mex.: University of New Mexico Press, 1987.

McKenna, James A. *Black Range Tales.* 1936. Reprint, Albuquerque, N. Mex.: Rio Grande Press, 1965.

Pattie, James Ohio. *The Personal Narrative of James O. Pattie.* 1931. Reprint, New York: Lippencott, 1962.

Pettitt, Roland A. *Exploring the Jemez Country.* Los Alamos, N. Mex.: Los Alamos Historical Society, 1990.

Pike, Zebulon. *The Journals of Zebulon Montgomery Pike.* Edited by Donald Jackson. Norman, Okla.: University of Oklahoma Press, 1966.

Reagan, A.B. "Geology of the Jemez-Albuquerque Region, New Mexico." *American Geologist* 31, no. 2 (1902):67–111.

Reeder, John D. "Faywood—A New Era." *New Mexico Magazine*, March 1982, 50–56.

Renick, B.C. *Geology and Ground Water Resources of Western Sandoval County, New Mexico.* Water Supply Paper 620. Washington, D.C.: U.S. Geological Survey, 1931.

Rieniets, Thomas Henry. "A History of the Montezuma Hot Springs, Hotels, and Bathhouses: 1840–1937." Master's thesis, New Mexico Highlands University, 1966.

Scholes, Frances V. "Notes on the Jemez Missions in the Seventeenth Century." *El Palacio* 44, no. 7 (1938):61–102.

Sierra County Historical Society. *History of Sierra County.* Truth or Consequences, N. Mex.: Sierra County Historical Society, 1979.

Simpson, James H. *Navaho Expedition: Journal of a Military Reconnaissance from Santa Fe, New Mexico, to the Navaho Country Made in 1849.* Edited by Frank McNitt. Norman, Okla.: University of Oklahoma Press, 1964.

Summers, W.K. *Catalog of Thermal Waters in New Mexico.* Socorro, N. Mex.: New Mexico Bureau of Mines and Minerals Resources, 1976.

Waters, Frank. *To Possess the Land: A Biography of Arthur Rochford Manby.* Chicago: Swallow Press, 1973.

Wechsberg, J. *The Lost World of the Great Spas.* New York: Harper and Row, 1979.

Whitehill, Betty H. "Tourist Mecca 1880 Style." *New Mexico Magazine,* June–July 1966, 18–19.

INDEX